Table of Contents

Forward: ....

Introduction: 5

Chapter One – One Man's Vision – A historical perspective [1] 10

Chapter Two – The year was 1999 13

Chapter Three - The year was 2000 19

Chapter Four – The Year was 2001 26

Chapter Five – The Year was 2002 38

Chapter Six – The Year was 2003 55

Chapter Seven – The year was 2004 76

Chapter Eight - Epilogue 81

Chapter Nine – Could the collapse have been prevented? 87

Chapter Ten – Lessons Learned 115

In Closing: 117

About the Author: 119

References and Endnotes 120

Key Officers, Executives and Managers 129

You decide the Collapse!

Thomas W. Szelinsky

Forward:

This book, *The Final Days of Weirton Steel*, is dedicated to a lot of people and hopefully I've touch on everyone in this forward. If I've missed someone I do apologize; it was not intentional.

I begin by dedicating this book first and foremost to my family, which includes my father Walter A., who provided 30 years of service, retiring in 1974 as a No. 5 Tandem Mill roller in the Strip Steel Department. We spent many a Sunday afternoon discussing (arguing) over what the final outcome would be for Weirton Steel. I guess I won. He died on January 4, 1999 never to see the final outcome, but I'm sure it would have broken his heart.

I also dedicate this book to:
- My beloved mother Walda A. whose career at Weirton Steel was short, not quite 9 months. She left after an accident when a pup coil fell on her foot in the assorting room of the Tin Mill. Pup coils are small coils that need special processing, each coil weighing several hundred pounds. Although she worked such a short time, she did manage to have her picture taken for the *Weirton Steel Bulletin*. Dad couldn't understand how that happened.
- My brother John R. who aspired to become Weirton Steel's best roller on the No. 2 Weirlite Mill in the Tin Mill, until an unfortunate non-mill related accident caused irreparable damage to his right ankle, prompting him to retire.
- My younger brother Don L. who worked only a few months after graduating high school and decided the mill wasn't for him.
- My wife Patricia E. for her 32 years of dedicated service to Weirton Steel and putting up with my erratic and sometimes impossible behavior over the last several years trying to put this material together. She aspired to be a highly refined and proficient electronic typesetter within Weirton Steel's Print Shop, retiring in 1999.

This book is especially dedicated to all the brave men and women and families of Weirton Steel that, through their combined dedication, sweat, tears, and sacrifice made Weirton a profitable and successful company; to all those employees who voted, with pride and confidence, that giving up nearly 32 percent of their wages and benefits would lead to job security for decades of future generations; to all of my uncles, aunts, cousins and close friends, many who are no longer with us and to all of my working associates from the Tin Mill and especially the Strip Steel, where I spent the early years of my career. This book is dedicated to all of you.

To all the employees of the Information Technology Department at Weirton Steel, before and after the ESOP, where I spent the final years of my career I dedicate this book to you. To each and every employee, you have my gratitude, respect and appreciation for all your hard work, dedication and sacrifice. You truly made a difference in what you did.

A special tribute goes to my good friend and colleague, Bernie Waters, who was tragically taken from us September 8, 1994 on USAir Fight 427. He would come into my office, sit down and would say, "Tom, what are we doing?" We would discuss whatever the situation was he had on his mind and usually have a laugh. He was an excellent sounding board and would always say what was on his mind and in his heart. He is often thought of and is sadly missed.

Last but not least I strongly acknowledge Weirton Steel, a company built on hard work, dedication and most importantly pride in quality; a company that set the example for the rest of the steel industry to take notice and always set the bar just a little bit higher; a company whose outstanding accomplishments led the way and set the pace and direction for the rest of the world's steel makers. I acknowledge all the extreme accomplishments and merits built by so many individuals only to see the company collapse at the hands of poor decision makers on the part of the board of directors, executive management, certain union officials, and our elected officials.

Some names of individuals have been intentionally left out unless those names were necessary to explain a particular circumstance. I left in titles so that the reader can appreciate at least whom I was dealing with. A list of names and titles can be found at the end of the book.

Introduction:

This book is based on my personal observations of daily, weekly and monthly events that led to Weirton Steel Corporation filing Chapter-11 bankruptcy on May 19, 2003. Data represented in this book is based from my personal record keeping of daily events, and from annual reports, proxy statements, and other data sources that pull and shape together my thoughts. These are also a gathering of my personal feelings, as I struggled to find answers to why the company got into this mess in the first place. It is a correlation of events and happenings, and about the people that I associated with that together tried to find remedies to prevent a bankruptcy from occurring in the first place. It is also a correlation of events and happenings and the people that, in my opinion, helped bring demise to this once great company.

You will learn how the board of directors failed in their duties as corporate overseers; learn how certain executive management individuals were allowed free reign and seldom held accountable for their decisions or their actions; learn how executives were rewarded for their lack of performance and negative business results; learn how the union failed to work alongside executive management to develop meaningful plans and solutions, especially during the period leading into and shortly after the bankruptcy; learn how our elected officials failed to respond toward company consolidation efforts; learn how the corporation was being run on a daily basis.

The Final Days of Weirton Steel are all the events presented in a monthly timeline leading up to the final sale to International Steel Group (ISG), which in my opinion, did not have to occur. The events and happenings that I'm about to describe are a combination of poor planning and poor decisions by the Board of Directors, and an unwillingness to work together between members of the Independent Steel Union and Weirton Steel's executive management team. They all contributed, in my opinion, to the collapse of Weirton Steel. I would be remiss not to include our congressional representatives from our great state of West Virginia in playing a part that guided Weirton Steel to its demise.

The series and sequences of events are important regarding the actions or inactions of how the company had been run prior to 1999 and up to the bankruptcy. Understand that despite incredible efforts, there were always some obstacles, real or imagined, that no one could move. Understand why the distractions from the steel industry as a whole, especially the large number of imports that flooded the market, were totally ignored until it was too late. Understand how the union decided to forego a management recommendation to forge a new company and ended new company negotiations on their own. You will see why so many key areas, and visible indicators, both inside and outside the company, were overlooked by the board, management, and the union until it was finally too late. You will understand how, all these events provided the means or the catalyst for the company to spiral needlessly and senselessly out of control.

There were a lot of very intelligent and dedicated people working at Weirton who stood by without raising their voices, knowing that if they did they would be out of a job; those voices will never be heard. There appeared to be some master plan that was being worked out that was impossible to stop. What went on in the various management meetings and board meetings were never fully disclosed to the public or the employees. It appeared in publication that the union and management were at odds with one another, but the actual story about the overwhelming animosity was never totally revealed.   This resentment or distrust not only existed between the union and executive management but also between individuals at the various levels of senior management as well.

The public was aware that Weirton Steel tried to consummate a deal to merge with Wheeling-Pittsburgh Steel, but were probably unaware that Weirton had spent our own money to secure financing that, in the final days, was all for not.   A complete reversal of those events could have happened, if only our elected officials were on the ball and understood what was truly at stake and had shown a genuine concern for the well being of Weirton Steel. As a union employee on the Stand Up For Steel site remarked, "Doesn't the government know we could shut down, we could all lose our jobs? Don't they care about us?" [1]

It is my view that a culmination of events and circumstances combined with poor decisions and a lack of accountability led to the failure of Weirton Steel but I'll let the reader decide. The contents of the book are facts as I recorded them, or specific detail as I researched them. This book encompasses the timeframe from 1999 to 2004, the period leading up to the bankruptcy and ultimate acquisition by International Steel Group. I conclude with a summary of "lessons learned" from this tragic event.

When someone entered into the work environment forty or more years ago their ultimate goal was to achieve "30-years" of service. That number was your "pot at the end of the rainbow," it was your "magic" number. Once you reached that milestone, you could decide if it was appropriate to actually retire. It was like earning a gold "badge" that had meaning and purpose; it was truly a mark of accomplishment.

If you did decide to retire, you would be able to retire with a pension, hopefully in a paid off home, so you could relax, travel, golf, or do anything your heart wanted as a reward for your years of dedicated service. There was this overwhelming sense of safety and security of having an income along with medical and life insurance. If, God forbid, anything did happen, you were certain that your family was provided for by the company you served for all those years.

I saw my father retire, not with very much, but enough to provide some happiness and contentment that enabled him and my mother to enjoy and do what they wanted. I saw my uncles and aunts retire and do exactly the same. They were able to relax and enjoy what their remaining years had to offer. These were people whose dedication was being rewarded, sometimes in only a small way, but nonetheless they were being taken care of for the balance of their lives without much worry. But that didn't happen for hundreds of employees at Weirton.

As I approached my "30-year" milestone I never expected to have the rug pulled out from under my feet, especially by a bankruptcy. But, when a bankruptcy hits, you feel a sudden panic pain and fear begins to overwhelm you with the realization that you're going to have to find a job; a life altering change because of major mistakes, poor decisions and a lack of accountability by those executives to whom we all trusted. The executives, on the other hand, were allowed to walk away, with huge sums of money, all set for life, at our expense. Somehow that just didn't seem fair.

In 2003, after the Pension Benefit Guarantee Corporation (PBGC) had taken over the pension plan, I contemplated what I would do next. I had 33 ½ years of service with Weirton Steel and with no other option available to me at that time, I decided to retire. I was given a pension at a mere fraction of what my entitlement was. From what little I was getting I had to pay for medical and life insurance because those were taken from us as well. I realized the inevitable, that I would have to find another job. I looked around and asked myself, "What the hell just happened?"

Let's take a look!

As I begin this journey, I am reminded and encouraged by the following:

Jesus said, "There is nothing hidden that will not become visible, and nothing secret that will not be known and come to light." Luke 8:17

"I am blessed because I seek refuge and put my trust in the Lord." Psalm 2:12

"Anyone can give up on anything at anytime, but true strength, without exception, is holding it together, through it all." Unknown

A special tribute to a very special friend for your spiritual inspiration and suggesting, "Maybe you should write a book," my heartfelt thanks: The Lord has truly blessed you and your family.

Chapter One – One Man's Vision – A historical perspective [1]

    The history of Weirton Steel Corporation is a classic story of true American ingenuity and entrepreneurial spirit. Weirton Steel was founded in 1909 by Ernest T. Weir, or E.T. to his friends. Mr. Weir, with wit, foresight and determination, built Weirton Steel into one of the world's leading steel manufacturing centers, a company founded on the principles of integrity, moral conviction, honesty and hard work where the reward equaled that of the sacrifice.

    The key to Mr. Weir's success was simple: invest in the company in good times, seize opportunity in tough times. He would hire and train the best while providing a decent wage and benefits. This was a solid formula that still works in today's society but only in the hands of the right people.

    Ernest T. Weir exemplified the self-made man. With only an eighth-grade education, Mr. Weir rose through the ranks of U.S. Steel Corporation, where he started as an office boy. By age 28, he was general manager of the Monessen tin plate mill near his hometown of Pittsburgh. In 1905, Mr. Weir took the chance of his life. He left a secure job of $5,000 per year, and with fellow employee James R. Phillips joined forces and ventured into business purchasing the Jackson Sheet and Tin Plate Company in Clarksburg, West Virginia.

    At this time John C. Williams, who had tin plate experience in Pittsburgh, joined Mr. Weir's enterprise. By 1908 the plant was operating extremely well, but it lacked the ability to move the finished material quickly or efficiently. Mr. Weir acted swiftly and searched for a new plant site, eventually selecting acreage on the Ohio River near the village of Holiday's Cove, (Weirton). Mr. Weir began building Weirton Steel in 1909 because the new site provided the abundant water supply needed, not only for steel production, but for transportation as well, allowing product to flow into major steel markets, which was something the Clarksburg facility couldn't provide.

    And so a new era of steelmaking began, forging nearly 80 years of remarkable success. A company built on a reputation of producing the highest quality steel in the world. Revolutionary efforts were realized from workers that came from all over the world. Weirton was a true leader of innovation in all areas of steel manufacturing and known specifically for its exceptional quality of "tin plate."

But on March 2, 1982, that historical journey was about to end. That particular day shocked not only the employees of Weirton Steel, but everyone across the Ohio Valley. On that day, National Steel made a devastating announcement; it decided to limit future capital investment in the Weirton division. However, National would be willing to discuss the option of the sale of the Weirton mill to its employees. A Joint Study Committee was formed and after 22 months of negotiations National Steel finally agreed to the terms and conditions of an Employee Stock Ownership Plan (ESOP).

On January 11, 1984, documents were signed between Mr. Howard P. Love of National Steel and Mr. Robert L. Loughhead, former Copperweld Steel president and now Weirton's new Chief Executive, forming the nations largest ESOP. Weirton Steel was about to charter another era of steelmaking.

In the 20 years that Weirton Steel existed as an ESOP, the company was able to earn an average of $1.2 billion in net sales per year. During that same 20 year period the company realized a net loss of nearly $1.5 billion. The largest losses came in 2001, 2002 and 2003.

Despite early ESOP success, Weirton required money for capital improvements, so in 1989, Weirton employees voted to relinquish some shares of the company stock in an initial public offering (IPO) to finance a five-year $740 million capital improvement program. A second IPO, in 1994, was necessary to shore up debt incurred in modernizing the plant. 2), 3), 4)

By 1996, with the debt reduced and the plant modernized, Weirton stood once again on firm financial footing, supposedly. However, the negative effects of a nationwide steel import crisis that supposedly began in 1998 had significantly reduced the company's production output, harmed its ability to control pricing and severely hampered its financial performance. Information derived from steel statistics, tracked from year to year, indicated the import crisis started way before 1998.

Weirton led the charge, along with other domestic steel companies for the U.S. government to uphold their federal trade laws regarding steel imports and the need to impose much needed tariffs. So going into 1999 Weirton had already lost $73.7 million. 5)

1999 would require extraordinary changes.

A detailed historical timeline of the company, along with important statistical data, can be found in the reference section. 2)

Chapter Two – The year was 1999

1999 brought with it sharply increased steel imports, up nearly 72 percent since November 1997. [1] A rally was being planned for January 20 in Washington, D.C. as a way for the government to see that this country needed someone to "Stand Up for Steel." But, why wasn't anyone in Washington observing what was happening? *What is it that our elected officials do there?* [2]

The biggest emphasis in 1999 was for companies all across the world to prepare for the Year 2000 computer fiasco that doomsayers predicted would cause a worldwide financial collapse due primarily to computers coming to a stop. Because this was such an important event, Weirton appointed one individual to oversee the entire process to ensure our computers would not stop working. This process was huge in every respect because of the hundreds upon hundreds of computer type devices that were inside the company. This meant any electronic device or computer that used a clock or date for daily operations had to be located and inventoried. We needed to know whether going from 1999 to 2000 if the computers were going to work properly; then we needed to have a plan developed to fix it, replace it, or eliminate it altogether. This entire plan was also designed to place the most critical items at the top of the list along with a timetable for not only completion but also testing to insure that everything was going to work when the clock changed.

The Information Technology Department and plant operations knew we were going to need a lot of help. Plans were generated so that money could be allocated to secure the resources needed to accomplish this monumental task.

Once the plan was prepared, monthly review sessions were conducted with the board of directors. Board meetings were conducted monthly and usually started at 8:30 a.m., and concluded between noon and 12:30 p.m. Normally, when presenting to the board, a certain amount of time was predetermined so that all the agenda topics could be covered within that four-hour window.

Those meetings were attended by me and presented by the Year 2000 project manager. This individual was selected because of his auditing background and because he was known for being very meticulous. The information presented not only included progress but roadblocks that might be of serious consequence to the corporation not meeting the deadline. Our allocated presentation time was usually ten but no more than 15 minutes. Generally, the allocated time was not sufficient because of the amount of material being presented and on the number of questions during the meeting.

What I thought very strange and very unprofessional was the mannerism of the Board Chairman. Mr. Richard R. Burt had replaced Mr. Herb Elish as chairman April 1, 1996. Mr. Richard K. Riederer had assumed the role of President, Chief Executive Officer and Chief Operating Officer. Mr. Burt had come to us from the Washington, DC area where he was Chairman of International Equity Partners, LLP.

I'm not sure what criteria the corporate search team used to select the chairman but something was missing in this person who represented the highest position within the corporation. His attitude and conduct at these meetings was not only rude it was to the point of being ridiculously obnoxious. This rudeness wasn't just to us who were presenting the Year 2000 information, but to nearly all those who had to make a presentation in front of this board.

You could tell by his mannerism that he was uninterested in the subject matter, especially the Year 2000 information. He would make gestures by rolling his hand as to say, "pick up the pace, it's approaching my lunch hour." I found his demeanor and disinterest one of the reasons the board failed to perform and why the executive management team was never truly held accountable. The board members should have demanded superior performance from the chairman, but that never happened. I'm guessing if the board members were on their game, the chairman and certain key executives would have been replaced, but that didn't happen either. So the work to prevent the Year 2000 "meltdown" continued.

In early February, Geneva Steel from Utah filed for Chapter-11 bankruptcy on the heels of Acme Steel from Riverdale, Illinois and Laclede Steel from St. Louis. It looked like the import crisis was starting to take its toll on some of the smaller companies. Weirton, trying to avoid a similar fate, decided to look at ways to reduce cost. One of the most effective and quickest ways was to reduce manpower.

So Weirton management began working on a plan for reducing the total staff, especially hourly employees. The company started the year with 4,329 employees and now was asking the union to reduce up to 370 employees for at least six months. Management and union agreed to reduce 231 senior hourly employees. There were a total of 800 hourly employees on lay off. In March, U.S. Senator Robert C. Byrd of West Virginia introduced a $1 billion Steel Loan Guarantee bill. This bill, would allow steel makers, if they qualified, to receive between $25 million to $250 million, with 85 percent of that money guaranteed by the federal government. The bill passed 289-141. Applications were now being accepted for any qualifying steel or manufacturing facility. By the end of March, Qualitech Steel Corporation, Pittsboro, Indiana and Worldclass Processing Corporation, Ambridge, Pennsylvania all filed for Chapter-11 bankruptcy.

The "Byrd Bill" as it became known was being scrutinized by Weirton as to the best possible use of those funds. A group of operations managers began looking into the possibility of a mini-mill and how it could complement our blast furnace production.

By mid-year some of the hourly employees returned to work, reducing the number of laid off employees to about 400. The government gave signs that it was seriously looking into the import crisis, and approved steps to place tariffs on steel. Gulf States Steel of Gadsden, Alabama filed for Chapter-11 bankruptcy.

As various groups within the management team looked at different strategies and opportunities, one came almost out of left field. It was suggested that I begin looking at exactly what it would take to merge Weirton and WHX Corporation, the parent company of Wheeling-Pittsburgh Steel Corporation. This was going to be a little difficult because I was asked to do it very discreetly. The sad part I was discouraged from getting any information from Wheeling-Pitt. *Okay, Houdini, do your stuff!*

My initial attempt was to tap my two trusted and loyal colleagues - - my faithful directors; Mike Biela and Dave Lammers. These two gentleman, each had a different area of responsibility and background. Mike on the application side and Dave on the infrastructure side, were unbeatable. I couldn't have performed my last couple of years at Weirton Steel without them. They were not only superior confidants but were always first to listen and then render comments and opinions. Mike was excellent at playing "devils advocate." He always would come up with different alternatives for us to consider. Dave on the other hand would always come up with different scenarios a day after our meetings. He needed time to grasp the situation and then would almost always have a couple of other options to explore. But, at the end of the day, we would always fully agree on our decision, and it would be my responsibility to deliver the outcome to either the employees or executive management. We were always in sync with the decisions we made and always our decisions were to keep the best interests of the employee and company in the forefront.

The meetings were held in strict confidence because any leak could have been disastrous to the corporation. Trying to curb rumors was a fulltime job, and we didn't need a big rumor to start; there was too much work to do. Working with my staff, our director of corporate strategy (since he worked at Wheeling-Pitt for a number of years) and the material supplied by a number of steel-related organizations, we were able to develop a broad sense of what Wheeling-Pittsburgh Steel had in terms of corporate computer systems and applications necessary to run one single corporation. We were progressing along nicely, but it was going to take more than what we had in order to put together a plan to present to the executive group. Then somehow the news broke about merger talks and everything changed. We now became inundated with more data then we could handle. After a couple of renditions we decided we had enough information so we could begin creating a model that would suggest some sense.

By mid-August nearly all the hourly employees were back on the job, and the market looked promising. In addition to the work on the Wheeling-Pittsburgh Steel merger, we were also in and out of meetings determining how best to apply for the money from the Byrd Bill.

A couple of business opportunities were beginning to get started for Weirton with hope that all would have successful outcomes. A new joint venture between Weirton Steel and ATAS International of Allentown, Pennsylvania to form W&A Manufacturing was beginning to take shape. W&A Manufacturing would manufacture and produce steel roofing panels and be marketed as the Advanta Shingle. This new product was developed at Weirton's WEIRTEC research and development facility as a result of the growth of metal products in the residential construction industry. It was part of Weirton's strategy to expand into value-added product markets. Product would be made from Weirton's hot-dipped galvanized material, a coated product with a fluoropolymer paint system for long-term durability. The product was available in six colors and had a 50-year limited warranty.

Also starting up at this time was Galvpro in Jeffersonville, Indiana. Galvpro was a new state-of-the-art hot-dip galvanize line expected to improve Weirton's overall galvanize market. This galvanizing joint venture was between Weirton and Royal Hoogovens and began operations in 1998.

By late October, it was pretty clear that all the work that had gone into the Wheeling-Pittsburgh Steel merger opportunity was now being put aside. Wheeling-Pittsburgh Steel posted a $4 million loss and all bets were now off. Over three months of intensive work was starting to collect dust.

In early December, MetalSite, a joint venture between Weirton Steel, LTV and Steel Dynamics, the second largest mini-mill in the United States was initiated to form an on-line electronic means to buy and sell steel using the Internet. Weirton Steel actually started this on-line electronic commerce initiative as an in-house project in 1996 and provided the initial "seed" money to get it up and operational.

This Internet website would not only list our secondary mill products but also those of other companies as well. *(Secondary product mix came in two forms: excess material that normally would be scrapped, recycled or sold; and excess prime material, which was a result of a perfectly fine coil somehow being partially damaged in the production process and unable to ship to the customer. Still considered prime material, it had to be reprocessed but sold at a lesser price. All this secondary material would be sold by our sales team but required a one-on-one approach which was extremely time-consuming and the results were not always positive in terms of getting the highest price.)*

However, having this secondary material posted on our internal website customers (who were previously approved for on-line bidding) could see what was available and then place their "bid" for the steel they wanted. This opened the door to allow a broader group to view our excess material eliminating the need for the "one-on-one" approach. This form of "blind" bidding always allowed Weirton to select and sell to the highest bidder, at the highest price. Weirton was now making money on product that usually was hard to sell and product that usually resulted in us practically giving it away. The thought process was to expand this technology concept as a private stand-alone enterprise.

MetalSite would be the first business-to-business e-commerce (electronic commerce) solution provider for steel products and was commissioned to go on-line in December. Despite a somewhat "shaky" start, the venture was kicked off with hopes of making lots of money.

Weirton had been struggling for months, and the financial outlook was bleak to say the least. Then before the end of December it was announced that Internet Capital Group (ICG) would pay some $180 million for a stake in MetalSite, and just like that, single handedly, that infusion of cash put Weirton Steel back into the black financially for the year. Weirton's No. 4 Blast Furnace was placed back on-line. The No. 4 furnace was the smallest of the blast furnaces and was used to compliment the output of the No. 1 furnace.

Investors at that time said they thought they had seen steel bottoming out and conditions starting to improve. The government stated there was evidence to support domestic steel industry claims that Japanese tin mill products were being dumped in the U.S. markets. It was reported that steel imports were down by nine percent. Everything appeared like a major turnaround for Weirton was starting to occur. If we could just clear the Year 2000 hurdle, it had the possibility of being a very good year.

Chapter Three - The year was 2000

Year 2000 came in like a lamb. All the doom and gloom reports that the "end" was coming or a "melt-down" would occur just didn't happen. With all the computer preparation and dedicated hard work of over 200 computer experts, the dividends paid off nicely and our computers rolled over into 2000 without any problems or issues. At twelve o'clock midnight, the lights didn't even flicker.

Early in January Weirton got a good boost from the financial world with an upgrade of our stock to a rating of 'B'. All the indicators from our internal financial people stated that it looked as though Weirton was out of the woods financially, at least for the time being, and that, fundamentally, businesses were starting to improve. We hoped the worst was behind us, especially financially, since Weirton had lost more than $50 million in the first three quarters of 1999. However we ended the year posting a $30.9 million profit. This came as a result of selling a portion of MetalSite shares and that allowed for a change in financial direction. If that sell off of MetalSite hadn't occurred, Weirton would have posted a loss of $76 million.

Some good news was reported. Not only did the company post a $30.9 million profit, but it also reported that the Weirton Pension Plan showed a surplus with assets of $790 million, $90 million more than the plan required. On a sour note however, the company reported no employer contributions to the Pension Plan were made in 1999. The $90 million surplus was the reason the company didn't add anything additional to the plan. The only negative news that started the year was the jobless rate had dropped to a 30-year low, and we saw a continuation of sell off of U.S. stocks.

By mid-first quarter, with the company once again on firm ground financially, it was reported that employees would be receiving profit sharing checks totaling some $5.5 million. Weirton's Executive Vice President of Operations, Craig T. Costello, reported that vast improvements in the plants performance through February had allowed many production units to operate at record levels and outperform certain business plan projections. That, in itself, was a total surprise.

Then a surprise announcement was made. Richard K. Riederer, President and Chief Executive Officer was stepping down as President, but would remain as the CEO. John H. Walker would replace Craig T. Costello and become the President and Chief Operating Officer (COO) effective March 21, 2000. Craig would retire effective April 1, 2000.

This move was completely unexpected especially from the mid-manager level. John H. Walker previously joined Weirton Steel in 1988 and was named executive assistant to the president. In 1989, he became director of operations planning before assuming subsequent positions as general manager of operations in 1994 and vice president of operations in 1995. John left Weirton Steel in 1996 and served as President of Flat Rolled Products and Vice President Operations at Kaiser Aluminum Corporation in Spokane, Washington until his return to Weirton in 2000.

Change at the top is never good unless there is a definite plan to turn a profit and make the necessary changes that will improve the overall performance of the company. Hopefully, John would be able to work with the board of directors and chairman, and make the necessary changes that I thought were so desperately needed. We certainly needed the board to place tighter reigns on executive management and their actions to achieve the performance goals they had set. My hope was John would work with those directors that had the interest of the company at heart and make the necessary changes.

Looking at the background of the board, it was apparent that the only board member at this time, who had an actual background in steel manufacturing, was D. Leonard Wise. The other members came from investment institutions, legal institutions, private enterprise or consulting firms. Without that steel manufacturing background one limits the ability to understand the elements that can affect decisions. It is sad that "Len" didn't come onto the board until the 1998 time frame; things just might have been different if he were there sooner.

The board of directors was highly profiled in Mr. Phillip H. Smith's book *Board Betrayal*. What many people, who read that book possibly didn't understand, was that the situation was worst then he portrayed and continued even after replacing the chairman. I'll elaborate more on the board in Chapter Nine.

As mentioned earlier, the selling off of U.S. stocks looked to be a problem toward the end of 1999 and into the early months of 2000. Then on April 5 the stock market took a major dive from 11,221 to 10,718 but managed to rally back to 11,164. Then by mid-month the Dow and

Nasdaq suffered an historic collapse. The Dow plunged 617 points to 10,305. Some good news was reported for Weirton, as first quarter results indicated we posted a small profit of $712,000 dollars.

Despite the collapse, or readjusting of the market, as some called it, business conditions appeared to improve only slightly. In early May, Weirton announced they were going to be hiring electrical and mechanical positions throughout the plant. However, on the down side, imports were being pushed to near record highs which meant more problems for the industry in general.

There was at this time, a major gathering of steel executives from across the entire steel industry meeting in Pittsburgh to discuss globalization of the steel industry. Then another surprise announcement occurred at the May board meeting when Dick Riederer stated he would be retiring at the end of year.

Dick Riederer had been the voice of the steel sector when it came to imports. He had an unquenchable passion not only to demonstrate that injury had occurred but also demanded that our nation's laws be upheld in any unfair trade of foreign imports. He had made it his quest for "zero tolerance" on unfair trade in the United States. Weirton did receive great news about an affirmative anti-dumping decision by the U.S. International Trade Commission (ITC), that duties up to 95% would be affixed on Japanese tin mill products (TMP) for the next five years. The punitive duty represents the amount the Commerce Department determined was the difference between the price Japanese exporters were charging customers in the United States, and the price they were charging in Japan for the same type of steel.

The Japanese steel industry issued a statement expressing bewilderment that the ITC, a U.S. government body, was not convinced by testimony from steel buyers, who said imports of the Japanese steel did not influence prices in the United States. It was a major victory for the U.S. steel industry and Dick Riederer to convince the ITC that harm did occur. I would be remiss not to acknowledge the gallant efforts of Independent Steel Union President Mark Glyptis for his spirited and dedicated efforts for lobbying on the behalf of steelworkers, not just at Weirton Steel, but for those steelworkers across the country, voicing his opinions to the ITC commission.

The corporation was active in the slight upswing of the business plan that allowed our operating units to exceed the plan. Others, like the project manager at WEIRTEC were working very diligently on developing a business model for a new venture: Polymer Coating.

Polymer Coating was developed at the Weirton Steel WEIRTEC research center. Polymer coating is applied, usually sprayed into cans after the cans have been formed but before food is placed into the container. Different coatings are applied depending on the type of food being placed into the can. There were nearly 150 different coatings within the industry. The Polymer Coating line and process would reduce the number of coatings to 25.

The polymer coating process would be applied to the coil before the coil was actually punched or was drawn into cans, thereby eliminating the cumbersome process of applying the coating after the can was already made. This was not only more efficient but would save money in processing time, and in the amount of polymer coating material used.

Weirton was looking at developing a business model that identified all the startup costs associated with a project of this size. A smaller polymer coating line, a demo line, was installed at the old Research and Development building behind the General Office building to test and prove the concept. With the concept proven, it was now ready for mainstream production.

By mid-July, companies who applied for the Byrd Bill were seeing results. WHX Corporation the parent company of Wheeling-Pittsburgh Steel Corporation received $35 million, Geneva Steel Corporation in Utah received $100 million and Northwestern Steel and Wire Corporation, in Illinois, received $170 million. Weirton was still in the running for a federal loan but to date hadn't received any notification regarding its application. On a sad note, J&L Structural Steel Inc., Aliquippa, Pennsylvania filed for Chapter-11 bankruptcy.

Weirton announced a modest profit for the second quarter of only $469,000. Our profit totaled about $1.2 million for the first half of 2000. Weirton's stock value at this point was $3.125 per share.

But even as somewhat positive announcements were being made, behind the scenes the markets were starting to show signs of slowing down. Dick Riederer, despite a victory on tinplate, continued his cry that steel imports were hurting and exploiting the industry. However,

Dick's reign was slowly coming to an end. As a result of the possible adverse effects of a slow market, Weirton Steel decided to put the electrical and mechanical hiring positions on hold, at least temporarily. The imports were really starting to affect industry jobs, but how long had the imports truly been a problem?

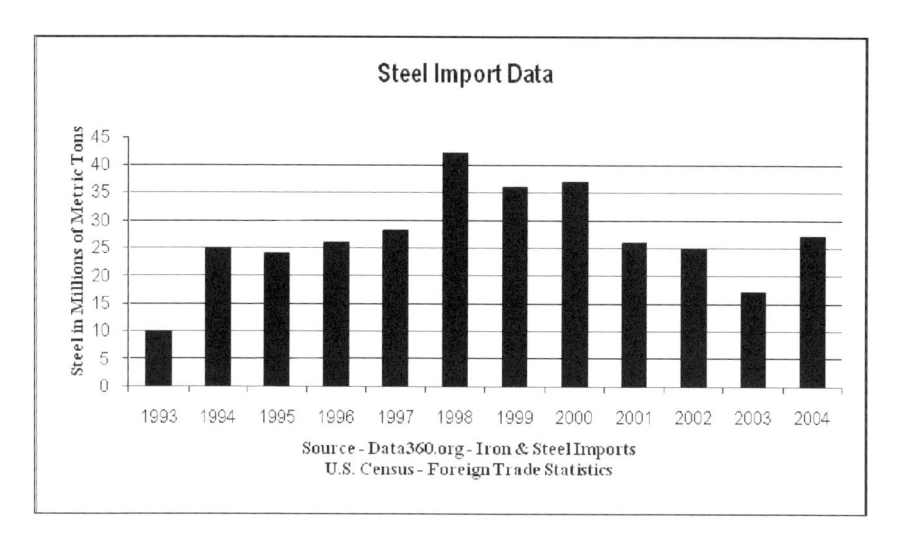

Steel Import Data

(Bar chart showing Steel in Millions of Metric Tons from 1993 to 2004)
Source - Data360.org - Iron & Steel Imports
U.S. Census - Foreign Trade Statistics

Looking at the graph [1] it appears that the imports started before 1993 and continued, unabated until the 1998 timeframe where they really spiked. If someone within Weirton Steel was keeping an eye on this situation, the company might have been able to react sooner and in a more positive manner. But, unfortunately that didn't occur, and the steel industry that this country counted on for over a hundred years was slowly sinking into extinction.

Our congressional officials in Washington didn't have their eye on this ball either. And even with the tariffs being applied in 1999, steel imports continued to be an issue. Unfortunately there are fewer steel companies around for the imports to affect.

In mid-September, I was asked to once again start looking at the possibility of a merger between Weirton and Wheeling-Pittsburgh Steel Corporation, and so the talks began. John Walker was now picking up the import fight, along with Dick Riederer. John wanted to keep pressure on import duties and not lose the momentum that Dick started. At the same time steel pricing started a downward spiral. More bad news came from the European stock markets as share prices fell dramatically. On the positive side, Weirton received news that it would receive a $25.5 million government loan from the Byrd Bill which would be used for general corporate purposes. We were hoping part of the money could be utilized for the Polymer Coating project. That idea was turned down by both executive management and the board of directors.

As we moved into the fall months, market conditions and the steel industry in general were showing signs that a deeper sag in the market was on the horizon. Stocks across Europe and the United States were down on news of the Yemen crises that began with hostile action to the USS Cole on October 12. Moreover, Weirton announced a third quarter loss of $26.2 million; it stated they were taking a write-off of $5.5 million for profit sharing and $6 million for the startup of Galvpro. In that short time frame of cautious optimism, the pendulum swung to the realization that things could get worse in a heart beat. The company also issued a warning about future earnings. We were facing reduced volume and the order book was off, at the same time imports continued to increase. At this point, Weirton decided to shut down its No. 1 Blast Furnace to help reduce inventory.

In November, Wheeling-Pittsburgh Steel reported it expected to post a loss of $21 million, and then a week later announced they were filing for Chapter-11 bankruptcy. This was on the heels of U.S. Steel and LTV Steel announcing layoffs of 120 and 80 employees, respectively. Announcements hit the papers that merger talks between Weirton and Wheeling-Pittsburgh Steel were back on, despite the bankruptcy filing of Wheeling-Pittsburgh Steel.

As the year 2000 slowly came to a close, 2001 didn't look one bit more promising. All the signs appeared that not only the steel industry, but also the country in general, was struggling and would continue to struggle into the foreseeable future. As Dick Riederer and John Walker kept up the fight for government assistance over imports, Wheeling-Pittsburgh Steel announced another 281 layoffs, bringing their total number of laid-off employees to 450.

Weirton Steel and the Independent Steel Union were beginning initial contract talks. The current 54-month union agreement was about to expire March 25, 2001. Weirton issued warnings to Wall Street about lower-than-expected earnings. Weirton Steel stock was now at an all time low of $1.50 per share.

As the year came to a close, it was apparent that more bankruptcies were imminent, not only by Wheeling-Pittsburgh Steel, but also by Vision Metals Inc., of Ann Arbor, Michigan, Northwestern Steel and Wire of Sterling, Illinois, Erie Forge & Steel, Erie, Pennsylvania, and LTV Steel Corporation, Cleveland, Ohio.

As peacefully as the year began we were now embarking on a journey into unchartered waters where the horizon was totally unclear, unsettling, and ominous. We needed to be prepared for the unexpected, but how do we do that? Never in Weirton's history had all the descending factors been so overwhelming and coming directly at the corporation at lightning speed. How could we brace for impact when you have never before been faced with so many events converging at the same time? *It was like being caught in the perfect storm.*

Chapter Four – The Year was 2001

The New Year was celebrated as usual with all the fan fair it deserved but those in the steel industry where not as joyous, only wishing for an up-swing in the market to help pull the industry up, or a reduction of imports, or some relief in pricing, anything, something! At this point, our legislators were becoming more vocal about the unfair dumping of steel into the country. John Walker applauded all the lawmakers for stepping up action against unfair trade. *What a surprise, something woke them up, but exactly what?*

The year started out with a small glimmer of good news. John H. Walker was named the new CEO of Weirton after being promoted from President and COO. John was a very intelligent and analytical individual, and I knew if anyone was going to take the helm and steady our course, John could do it. We all needed to do more than we had ever done before and stand firmly behind him and give him all the support we could muster. Unfortunately, since John arrived, little had changed in terms of accountability. *This was probably not a good time for changing key personnel since the house was crumbling around us, but it certainly needed a thorough sweeping.*

Good news for Laclede Steel in Illinois, and Geneva Steel in Utah, as both companies emerged from bankruptcy. However, on the downside, United Steelworkers of America President George Becker offered a sobering point of view. He stated the future looked dire and asked for a $10 per ton import tax on all steel products. Within two weeks after the beginning of the year there was another fatality, as CSC Ltd., of Warren, Ohio, filed for Chapter-11 bankruptcy protection.

As the month slowly unfolded, Weirton Steel announced a fourth quarter 2000 loss of $60 million while posting an $85.1 million loss for the year 2000. Weirton stated that unfair imports kept selling prices in decline during most of the year. Compounding the import problem was a slowing economy and higher energy costs. Imports for 2000 were 37.8 million tons, just under the record 1998 year of 41.5 million tons.

By the end of January, Heartland Steel Inc., of Terre Haute, Indiana filed for Chapter-11 bankruptcy. They were later sold to CSN of Brazil. Qualitech Steel SBQ, LLC of Indiana ceased operations all together. Nucor Steel was willing to pick up all their assets.

In early February, I was asked to deliver a proposal to executive management, for more job eliminations and come up with additional cost reductions. At this time, the "Year 2000" activities were behind us and left the Information Technology Department (IT) with a total staff of 153 employees. The staff consisted of 85 contract employees and 68 Weirton salary exempt employees. We needed to reduce that number to a more practical and realistic level. Our emphasis was on maintaining a high level of customer service satisfaction, not only for the corporation as a whole but to our outside customers as well.

By the beginning of January 2001, we had reduced 31 contract employees that realized an annualized savings of $2.7 million. We also had, during that timeframe, two Weirton employees resigned, leaving a department of 120. It was comprised of 54 contract employees and 66 Weirton salaried employees.

The task of reducing further jobs came as no surprise to me. In fact that was probably the biggest part of my job: reducing people and looking for ways to reduce costs. The IT Department already had plans underway not just to reduce jobs, but to streamline the department in general to make it more cost-efficient, even before the directive was issued. My philosophy had always been to salvage as many Weirton employee jobs and reduce outside contractors by shifting the work and responsibilities over to the Weirton employees. So, working in almost daily meetings, behind closed doors and many times after hours, so as not to draw suspicion to our efforts, my directors and I agreed on not only a reduction in contractors but to achieve combined cost savings totaling $3.5 million as well.

This proposal was then reviewed with my superior, the Chief Financial Officer, Mark Kaplan. He agreed that the proposal was solid, the numbers realistic and transfer of responsibility a possibility. He also welcomed the $3.5 million in annualized savings. Every little bit helped.

I met several days later with our new President John Walker, the Vice President of Human Resources and Legal, and my Human Resources representative to go over my proposal. I considered one of my main strengths to be thoroughness when it came to detail. I wanted to make sure whatever I presented there was always sufficient documentation behind the information. Likewise for this meeting, I came prepared with more than enough documentation so a thorough understanding of the cost reductions and manpower changes could take place in the shortest timeframe, and thus provide the greatest benefit to the company.

After presenting the information, the Vice President indicated that this was just more information than they needed. He asked me if I knew the importance of the exercise I just completed and I replied that I did. After all, I had just the day before reviewed the information with the CFO, and he gave his blessing for me to review this information with the president. I was then informed that the exercise wasn't about contractors or cost savings, but the reduction of Weirton Steel salary employees. I had to admit that I was unaware of the need to permanently reduce out salaried employees; if this were the case I would have assumed that the CFO would have told me. This information came as a complete surprise.

John Walker then informed me to go back and cut 13 salaried people from my department, in addition to what I was already proposing. I was stunned and amazed at the suggestion. He didn't even think of any impact or possible side effects that reducing 13 salary employees would cause to the services being provided by the IT Department. It was just a definitive, emphatic 13 people; case closed. The Vice President even challenged me with names of certain individuals to consider. With that said, the Vice President indicated that the information I presented should be "shredded." He asked that we each pass our presentation copies to the Human Resource representative, and he was told to shred them. I was then instructed to get the copy given to the CFO and shred that copy along with deleting any files on my computer required to prepare the proposal I had just presented.

I left the meeting and walked to the CFO's office and asked him if he knew of reducing salary employees. He said he did not know, or at least didn't realize that was what was being asked. I suggested he should talk to John so everyone was on the same page because this was a little embarrassing. I walked out of his office quite dismayed, but that was common, it was a way of doing business at Weirton Steel. *It seemed the right hand didn't always know what the left hand was doing, especially when dealing with some executives.*

I sat in my office for probably 30 minutes or more contemplating what my next move was going to be. How was I going to eliminate so many dedicated employees, and without them knowing what was going on? So, I gathered my two directors and explained that we didn't do as good of a job on the proposal as we had thought. I explained what we now needed to do and the urgency of getting it done. Another trait at Weirton was everything was an emergency and required being done yesterday. I remember the old adage that "poor planning on your part doesn't constitute an emergency on mine," but nonetheless we needed to get something started.

We began meeting away from my office to begin the difficult task of eliminating 13 salaried employees. These employees had given and sacrificed a great deal for the good of Weirton Steel, and now we needed to sort through them like cattle going to the slaughter. These individuals also thought they would ultimately see their 30-year milestone. You needed to understand that the Information Technology Department was like the electric company. No one knows you're there or what you do until the lights go out, and then they come unglued like it was the end of time. *And so our work began.*

As we moved through the month of February, Weirton saw an increase in order book volume and decided to restart the No. 4 Blast Furnace. This was possibly the shot in the arm the company needed to offset the previous month's spoils. Only one company filed for Chapter-11 bankruptcy, GS Industries of Charlotte, North Carolina. Senator Robert C. Byrd cried that unfair trade was crippling the steel industry, and the government was doing nothing to offset the problem. The month brought some decline in imports but really not enough to start a turnaround. Weirton's stock had fallen to $1.00 per share.

Since the Steel Loan Board became active for the steel industry it had given out 13 loans totaling $901 million. The following distribution of money occurred; ($170 million) Northwestern Steel & Wire, Illinois; ($110 million) Geneva Steel, Utah; ($100 million) Acme Steel, Illinois; ($60 million) CSC Ltd, Ohio; ($50 million) GS Technologies, North Carolina; ($35 million) Wheeling-Pittsburgh Steel, West Virginia; and ($25.5 million) Weirton Steel Corporation, West Virginia.

Weirton Steel officials and union leaders continued to negotiate terms and conditions for a new union contract. The issues were typical of union contracts: pensions, health care and job security were the greatest concerns. However, the contract's main issues hadn't yet been addressed.

Meanwhile, I was struggling not only to come up with a logical and ethical way of permanently reducing 13 salaried employees, but also working on a systematic plan to merge two antiquated steel companies. The trick here was to merge the complex antiquated companies and computer systems while not losing one dollar of revenue or one ton of material (inventory).

At the same time, my two directors and I put together a plan that we thought might help several of the more senior staff personnel by offering them some type of enhanced retirement. However, that plan wouldn't work for some of the middle management staff. How were we going to do this elimination? It became extremely difficult. But, we put our list together anyway, and with much pain and reluctance, I presented our suggestions to my Human Resource representative. I had asked repeatedly, after that day, as to when the eliminations might be expected, but the answer was always the same: "we don't know."

Then on Thursday, March 15, my Human Resources representative came into my office with a stack of folders. In the conference room next to my office sat a representative for "outplacement" services and the worst day of my life began to unfold. This event was totally unexpected until about an hour before the task was to take place. I was asked to call each person in and follow the instructions I was provided.

As I called the first person into my office, she knocked on the door, and as she entered I noticed a notepad and pencil. She obviously thought she was getting an assignment to work on. Little did she realize that she would not need to write a single word on her notepad; she was being handed a packet of information that represented her termination. I remember having to read that pre-written statement that was all too cold, and those words resonated in my office. I was, for the first time in my career, ashamed of what I was doing. After the first person left and was introduced to the lady next door, I called in the next, and then the next, until a total of twelve were processed. I was numb after the first and stayed that way for the next four days. The 13th person was processed the next day.

I really don't know how I stayed composed or didn't get emotional, because my heart ached, and it was if I had just been beaten to an inch of my life. Every muscle in my body felt like rubber, and nothing I could think of could make me smile or think of something pleasant. Everything was dark.

I can still see the faces of each and every person I talked to that day and I'll probably keep those images all the rest of my days. How cold and impersonal that entire process was. We couldn't answer any questions. Answers to any question could be taken out of context and used in an employee's lawsuit, if they chose to pursue a legal challenge. My management style of open door, you can talk to me about anything, I am easy to work with, was gone. I was now and forever more, the most hated person in Weirton Steel, especially to the 13 people in the IT Department. That was a department that we all contributed to and developed together. It was a department, that if I had to relive my career over, I would pick. Everyone had a personal talent that they used every day to help benefit Weirton Steel, some maybe more than others, but nonetheless everyone contributed something. I also believe that your success can be made by surrounding yourself with people who can offer strengths to your weaknesses, and collectively, you can accomplish almost anything. Our IT Department could accomplish just about anything.

I left that day with the heaviest heart I have ever had. I didn't feel that low, sad and hurt when my parents died. There had to be a better way. I wasn't the only one passing out bad news that day. In fact, Weirton cut 70 salary management jobs that day citing that current economic conditions that led to the decision. The depressing part of that most horrific exercise was that not one executive had to do what I just did. Not one executive had to look into the face of that employee being terminated. How sad! At this point we had approximately 630 salaried employees and 3500 unionized workers left.

The first quarter came to a close with the U.S. stock market falling below 10,000 points, and the Asian markets slid backwards as well. Weirton's stock was selling for 99 cents a share. Trico Steel of Decatur, Alabama and American Iron Reduction of Convert, Louisiana both filed for Chapter-11 bankruptcy. Weirton and the ISU agreed to extend the existing contract for 70 days. They indicated that wage and pension improvements would be made retroactive. Decisions were not coming easy, and when there was a lull, that always meant no decisions.

As soon as April started it was announced that Republic Technologies of Akron, Ohio filed for Chapter-11 bankruptcy. There appeared to be a trend to what was happening in the steel industry. A watchful eye behind the scene here at Weirton told me that Weirton would be in serious trouble if steps weren't taken soon. Weirton and the ISU began talking about the big-ticket issues for a new contract. These appeared to be very complex and centered on job security, pensions and benefits. Just about every steel company in America either filed for bankruptcy, or was preparing to file for bankruptcy, and the union was worried about job security, pensions and benefits.

Then came a surprise as Wheeling-Pittsburgh Steel Corporation announced losses for 2000 totaling $181 million. Weirton Steel announced it lost $75 million in the first quarter. Of the $75 million loss, $12 million was for restructuring costs for management layoffs and $19 million for operations at Galvpro. In essence, Weirton actually lost $44 million in the first quarter. The company sited a lack of action by the government to prevent imports despite reports that showed imports beginning to drop as the demand for steel began to shrink. With $19 million going for the operations at Galvpro it didn't appear that the facility would be around much longer. Before the month ended, Great Lakes Metals of East Chicago and Algoma Steel in Canada, both announced filing for Chapter 11 bankruptcy. Weirton's stock was now selling at 77 cents a share.

The month of May began with a tentative agreement being reach with the ISU. Terms of the new 15-month union contract included no pay raise, but did include provisions to maintain health care benefits and enhancements to the pension fund. The Union was trying to establish a quick ratification. As a result of the management reductions in March, a class action lawsuit by 12 of the 70 employees was filed. *Way to go, nothing to lose, everything to gain.*

The sad part about that statement was Weirton never, never learned from their mistakes when handling or dealing with layoffs and terminations. Every time the employees who sued won, and won big time. And yet another round of law suits coming up and if I had been a betting person, I would have bet these individuals would walk away with plenty.

It was also announced that Dick Riederer former President and CEO had earned $2.3 million dollars after stepping down. Union leadership was up in arms regarding the amount since the company was heading into a downward spiral. A call for a "Section 201" [1] probe was seen as positive news. However, on the downside Northwestern Steel and Wire, already in bankruptcy, suspended their operations.

The month of June started off with President George H.W. Bush ordering a probe into the massive number of imports coming into the United States. Weirton elected to shut down the No. 4 Blast Furnace for a period of 10-12 weeks in order to reduce inventory. The Independent Steel Workers Union ratified a new 15-month labor contract. And as if the events unfolding at Weirton couldn't get worse, they did. MetalSite, the on-line marketplace for steel products, announced they were suspending operations effective immediately. Weirton's stock price also took a nosedive closing at only 68 cents per share.

The month of July began with all employees, except those required to maintain certain critical operations, taking a mandatory one-week vacation. As employees came back from vacation, it was announced that Weirton Steel was embarking on a companywide cost savings program. It consisted of three main steps;
1) To maintain the company as a long-term viable entity,
2) To protect pension and healthcare benefits for all active and retired employees, and
3) To maintain the community standard of living. Some $10 million in savings had already been identified and not all as a result of job cuts. *Here we go, setting more goals and achieving very little.*

So, we started on a comprehensive exercise that was to leave no stone unturned. As we looked at new ways to reduce IT Department costs, I knew we were on the right track when our analysis began to make us feel uncomfortable. I needed to move people out of their respective comfort zones. Saying something wouldn't work was totally unacceptable. Once we all moved away from our pigeonholes, new ideas gave way and costs started to come down. But if costs came down the overall quality of service we provided to our internal and external customers had to improve. That was the IT challenge.

July also saw Freedom Forge (Standard Steel's parent company) of Burnham, Pennsylvania, Excaliber Holding Corporation of St. Louis and

Precision Metals of Los Angeles became the nineteenth company to succumb to foreign imports, all having to address reorganizations. Laclede Steel of St. Louis was forced to re-file for bankruptcy protection, a mere seven months since emerging from the last bankruptcy.

The month of August saw steel imports continue to climb. The first six months of 2001, imports were 14.1 million tons, down thirty percent, but in June had increased nearly ten percent. Not totally unexpected, Weirton announced a second quarter loss of $64.1 million. *We just couldn't stop the bleeding.*

Similar to previous months, the trend continued as Edgewater Steel of Oakmont, Pennsylvania, and Riverview Steel Corporation of Glassport, Pennsylvania filed Chapter-11 bankruptcies. On August 10, GalvPro of Jeffersonville, Indiana, a galvanizing joint venture with Weirton and Royal Hoogovens, that began operations in 1998, filed for Chapter-11 bankruptcy protection.

Cost-saving program initiatives and ideas continued almost daily with additional suggestions and ideas flowing all over. These were extremely bad times that called for us to try anything and everything. A new union labor agreement was put into place. In addition to the labor contract there was an agreed reduction in management staff and other employment costs relating to exempt compensation. An agreement in principle with certain key vendors to provide the company with additional liquidity was also being put into place, as well as a signed commitment letter from a financial institution that would enable the company to restructure its current working capital facilities. Generating ideas and creating goals was always an easy task, the hardest part was succeeding in getting them implemented.

The new union labor contract called for approximately 446 job eliminations; 372 coming from the production area, and 74 coming from the salary non-exempt area. The employees that were left in these affected areas would assume additional responsibilities. Those individuals would be eligible for a wage increase in 2003.

But Weirton received more bad news as the New York Stock Exchange announced it was suspending trading of Weirton Steel stock. Our stock was selling for only 25 cent per share. *This was not generally a good sign of things to come.*

In September, Weirton stock began trading over-the-counter with the symbol WRTL. Then the massive devastation of New York City took place, on September 11, as terrorists used our own airplanes to bring down the Twin Towers of the World Trade Centers. The stock market plummeted after the terror attack leaving complete uncertainty of how the country would survive. Despite the feelings of being violated by the 9/11 attacks, the work to keep Weirton afloat still had to be done. Not only were cost-cutting proposals being generated, the IT Department also launched an effort to bring costs down through our vendor community. We embarked on contacting every single vendor and either they reduced their costs, or we found a way to eliminate their service from the company. In other words, either you help save the company, or we don't need your services anymore.

In early October, Weirton was joined by seven other steel companies and filed trade lawsuits. On October 15, Bethlehem Steel Corporation filed Chapter-11 bankruptcy protection. Acme Metals who was in the process of reorganization, announced that they were beginning a phased shutdown of their operating facilities and liquidating their assets.

About mid-October, under the new leadership of President John H. Walker and CFO Mark Kaplan, Weirton announced it was going to prepare an "out-of-court reorganization" plan. Plans were being made by every department within Weirton to begin aggressive cost reduction opportunities and to start thinking "outside the box." No one had to tell us to think outside the box because we were brainstorming every conceivable idea imaginable. Either we do this reorganization plan now, or we do it under Chapter-11, but it had to be done, regardless. *Let's switch directions and come at this from another angle and different goals.*

On October 21, the Section 201 investigation by the ITC (International Trade Commission) found that U.S. steel producers had been injured by a continuing surge of low priced imports over a broad range of products. Entering the remedy phase of the Section 201 investigation, the ITC now had 60 days to develop and present remedies for President Bush to consider in dealing with the imports. *Maybe just a little too late. Why does it take so long for something to happen in Washington?* More bad new came as Weirton announced a third quarter loss of $60.2 million.

In early November after many long months of cost reduction efforts, it appeared that some of those efforts were starting to show signs of working. Weirton announced a new $200 million credit facility along with lending companies, CIT Group/Business Credit, Inc., GMAC Business Credit, and Transamerica Business Capital Corporation. No. 9 Tandem Mill and our Hot Strip Mill were used as collateral to secure the financing.

The month of November was a very busy month. We needed to finalize the strategic "out-of-court reorganization" plan and prepare to deliver that plan to the board of directors at the next meeting. The plan consisted of two strategic objectives;

1) Tactical/Restructuring, namely implement a new labor package, additional exempt reductions, a vendor liquidity program, a new senior credit facility and a successful exchange offer, and
2) Fundamentally reposition the company.

Completing these two objectives would guarantee Weirton long-term profitability and viability, or so it was perceived. These were not easy objectives by any stretch of the imagination. The other less likely objective was to be acquired by some outside organization. *Here we go again, more goal setting; if at first you don't succeed!*

At this point in time, the only two domestic interests that showed any interest in Weirton were U.S. Steel and Nucor Steel, but their interest didn't appear sincere. On the foreign side, the Japanese showed no interest because they were having their own similar problems. The European community was primarily looking at partnering with a Tier I mill and Weirton did not fit that picture. Latin America, namely CSN from Brazil had expressed some interest but not enough to place any hope with finding a quick solution to our dilemma.

So our two-prong strategic plan was ready to present to the board of directors. However, on November 14, Metals USA of Houston, Texas filed for Chapter-11 bankruptcy protection.

As another year was slowly coming to an end, the month of December saw Sheffield Steel of Sand Springs, Oklahoma and Action Steel Incorporated of Indianapolis, Indiana file for Chapter-11 bankruptcy protection. The former LTV Steel Corporation stopped making steel and began a liquidation of their assets.

Every direct report from every key department was feverishly working to establish a baseline for the restructuring plan to kick-off 2002. The 2002 Business Plan reflected nine major assumptions:
1) Liquidity is tight with a dip after the February vacation pay out and a low point in May, after which it was predicted to rise through the rest of the year,
2) EBITDA (Earning Before Interest Taxes, and Depreciation) would turn positive in the second half of the year,
3) The Plan reflects a successful bond exchange,
4) Operational cost savings will be in full swing in the second quarter,
5) Hot Mill is at full capacity, the finishing and primary production is up from 2001,
6) A strong price recovery in the sheet metal market was expected,
7) Shipping volume would increase,
8) Developing a richer product mix; tin plate and galvanize volumes would increase, and seconds and excess material volumes expected to decline, and finally, and
9) Lower raw material and energy costs, led by natural gas. If these assumptions all come together Weirton could stay afloat a little while longer. [2] *How much longer, no one knows.*

Chapter Five – The Year was 2002

January got off to a roaring start with the board of directors approving the restructuring plan. On January 16, President John Walker made a management presentation that outlined the restructuring plan to all management employees. The plan had a little more detail than the plan presented to the board in November.

The Restructuring Plan Detail [1] was as follows:
1. Growing Tin and selected Sheet Product
    a. Acquisition and organic growth in tin products
    b. Shrink sheet, while targeting smaller, more profitable sheet accounts/niche segments
    c. Optimize galvanizing capabilities
    d. Commercialize Polymer Coating
2. Financial Goals – To improve the company's near term liquidity by a minimum of $100 million
    a. Company wage earners/cost reduction initiative – $40 million
    b. Vendor Liquidity – $30 million
    c. New Credit Facility – $35 million
    d. Debt Restructuring – $30 million
        i. Total Liquidity Improvement $135 million.
3. Exempt Wage and Benefit Costs
    a. Elimination of 100 exempt positions
    b. Senior Management Team Contribution
    c. Reduction of outside contractors
    d. Compensation frozen through first quarter of 2003
4. Collective Bargaining Agreements
    a. Term – March 31, 2004
    b. Reduction in employment by attrition and targeted early retirement
        i. Production and maintenance – 372
        ii. Office clerical and technical – 78
    c. Compensation
        i. Shared savings

ii. Wage increase of $1.00 per hour effective April 1, 2003
5. Other Company Wide Savings
    a. Central Machine Shop – $3.1 million
    b. Building Consolidation – $1.2 million
    c. Blue Cross Administrative Costs – $3.0 million
    d. Other Identified Projects – $2.7 million
        i. Total Savings – $10 million.
6. Vendor Liquidity Programs – 62 vendors participating, which represents 45% of the total spend
    a. Foster-Wheeler Sale and Leaseback – $25.6 million
    b. General Office and R&D Sale and Leaseback – $3.0 million
    c. Vendor Price Concessions – $1.7 million
    d. Other, principally consignment arrangements – $1.9 million
        i. Total Vendor Liquidity Programs – $32.2 million.
7. Senior Credit Facility – replaces current working capital facilities and creates additional borrowing capacity of $35-40 million.
    a. Fleet Capital Corporation – $50.0 million
    b. Foothill Capital Corporation – $50.0 million
    c. CIT Group/Business Credit, Inc. – $50.0 million
    d. GMAC Business Credit LLC – $35 million
    e. Transamerica – $15.0 million
        i. Total Senior Credit Facility – $200.0 million.

This restructuring plan was very aggressive but also very doable, and it absolutely had to all come together to maintain Weirton as a viable steel company. We truly had to keep our head above water, at least until things started to improve, but no one knew for how long. We really needed to start not only achieving our goals but surpassing them. We really needed to see success from the sales and operations groups, as well as all the other ancillary areas in the company. On the positive side of operations, the No. 4 Blast Furnace was once again placed back on-line and into full production.

As January came to a close and February began, it appeared as though we were moving forward with achieving some of our objectives.

However, Weirton reported a staggering fourth quarter loss of $180 million and a net lost of $533 million for the year. That number was just too big to fully digest, but with that said, the restructuring plan was now more important than ever to complete, and if possible, exceed. *The blood continues to flow and now more abundantly.* Huntco Inc., of Town and Country, Missouri filed for Chapter-11 bankruptcy and ceased operations.

A massive postcard effort was initiated to have every able-bodied person send notice to Washington, as a wake-up call to what was happening to our once strong and vibrant steel industry. By month's-end, employees boarded buses and headed to Washington, D.C., for another rally to bring focus on the industry. *What's happening in the offices of Rockefeller, Byrd and Mollohan? Do these elected officials know of our struggling problems?*

Some good news was realized as Weirton announced that agreement was reached on the restructuring plan. More importantly, news came on February 20 that the ITC voted unanimously that unfairly traded stainless steel bar imports from five countries had injured the U.S. steel industry. As a result, importers from France, German, Italy, South Korea and the United Kingdom had to continue to pay duties of as much as twelve percent on stainless steel. *What have our congressional officials been doing?*

Unsuspecting to the steel industry as a whole, a fox was about to emerge and begin a massive feast. In the months that closed 2001, and into the New Year, a new company was being formed that some would consider a "knight in shining armor." But for some, however, this was a fox that would devour the less fortunate bankrupt steel companies.

In February, it was made public that a new company was formed called International Steel Group (ISG) headed up by businessman Mr. Wilbur L. Ross. His mission was to seek out and buy bankrupt steel companies, but only those that could turn an immediate profit. While all the other steel companies were busy contemplating a strategy to avoid bankruptcy, Mr. Ross was quietly shopping for the best assets on the market. Mr. Ross lay waiting in the background, and without fanfare began buying up bankrupt steel companies starting with the LTV Steel Company based in Cleveland, Ohio. ISG became the only bidder of the liquidated company consuming the remnants for $325 million.

This acquisition, however, wasn't the typical purchase of a bankrupt steel mill. Something was drastically missing. Since the company was liquidated, Mr. Ross did not have to assume any of the legacy obligations namely health care, insurance and pension benefits promised to legions of retirees. Mr. Ross thought he could remake the steel industry by circumventing the high labor and legacy costs.

Mr. Ross' deal looked even better a few weeks later, when the Bush administration, eager to provide some relief to the battered steel industry, announced in early March a 30 percent tariff on many types of imported steel. It was again a victory for the steel industry, but maybe a little too late. The Bush administration announced a temporary safeguard, a program of tariffs on steel imports to be applied over the next three years. These safeguards were the result of the ITC's investigation into the impact of imports on the U.S. steel industry under Section 201 of the 1974 Trade Act. The ITC commissioners had delivered their recommendations in December 2001, concluding the second phase of the ITC's investigation. Five of the six ITC commissioners recommended that President Bush impose tariffs for four years on 16 types of steel products. The three-year package of penalties ranged between 8-30 percent and would take effect on March 20.

Suddenly, LTV, now renamed ISG, looked like it could be a very vibrant steel concern. It rehired about 60 percent of LTV's employees and started making steel again. Making steel again, something that no one, a few months earlier, would have ever dreamed possible. It was happening and with a significant lower cost structure. Mr. Ross proclaimed his intention to reduce the number of man-hours required to produce a ton of steel by nearly 70 percent. As this all came about the former employees found something drastically different. First, the employees, before being hired, were screened as they returned to their respective jobs. It was almost as if they were being hand selected. They were negotiating with a fresh perspective. ISG replaced lifetime pension and health-care benefits with a 401(k), and a tentative deal to tie other benefits to company and individual work performance. The employees were now going to operate under new work rules, driving responsibility for performance directly into their hands. Workers received extra pay for beating production goals, a rarity under prior union contracts. *What a marvelous idea!*

Still the rest of the unsuspecting steel industry really didn't pay that much attention to what was happening at ISG. And so, this Mr. Ross, head of W. L. Ross & Company out of New York, bought a dilapidated steel plant, so what!

Then on March 6, amazing word came down that none other than National Steel Corporation of Mishawaka, Indiana had filed Chapter-11 bankruptcy. The former parent company of Weirton, this colossal giant, National Steel was in serious financial trouble. It was truly hard to imagine. Calumet Steel of Chicago Heights, Illinois filed Chapter-11 bankruptcy and ceased operations as well.

The months of April and May proved to be quite stressful as vendor meetings occurred to reduce their costs, while still providing the same or improved level of service. It was also stressful because we, within the IT Department, labored over how many employees and contractors we could eliminate and still keep the wheels on the bus. As I look back on all we did it reminded me of at least 50 some scenarios that developed. *The long hours and sleepless nights were beginning to take their toll.*

What made these extremely difficult times was the plain and simple fact that the people we were discussing were our colleagues and our friends. This was especially true for our co-workers, the Weirton employees whom we had known for decades. Their families, their children, -- their lives were in my hand and the hands of my two directors. We were about to change their lives and futures in a very profound and sad way.

We were involved in a similar analysis nearly 18-months earlier, and one would have thought we would be somewhat hardened to this process by now. But, when you deal with people's lives and the fate of their futures, and their inability to provide for their families, it is never an easy task; it is truly painful and extremely unpleasant. It was probably the most difficult and the hardest undertaking I ever went through, aside from the task of dismissing twelve IT employees in a single day. You try to convince yourself that in order for this company to succeed, to survive, you have to sacrifice your job. Now as I put these words to print, it somehow doesn't make any sense at all. It almost sounds ludicrous. But the task had to be completed, if not by my direct reports or me, then by someone else who might not have understood the personal and sensitive implications of this most difficult process.

In May, we received more disappointing news. The company announced a $44.6 million loss for the first quarter. What we thought we were going to get from our efforts was apparently not showing up on the bottom line, and time was quickly running out.

In spite of everyone's efforts, we never seemed to realize any of our goals. I contribute those unrealized goals to a lack of initiative on management's part along with poor leadership in demanding the goals be achieved. No one in executive management ever put the hammer down. They never discarded the "rotten apple from the barrel." They just tolerated the smell and kept going.

I felt that the sales and manufacturing areas needed to experience a leadership change. If we stood any chance at all to realize our goals, we needed to change the leadership in those two areas. Simply put, those guys talked a good talk but failed to produce, and always had an excuse for why goals couldn't be reached.

Daily performance meetings were not giving way to what company officials had hoped to accomplish. However, the effort on the strategic plan was struggling at best but kept moving forward ever so slowly. A couple of major developments occurred, one particularly in the exchange offerings. We completed the bond exchange totaling $300 million. As a result of exchange offers, the company would reduce leverage by approximately $115 million in indebtedness by exchanging $261 million of its outstanding debt for $146 million of new secured notes and shares.

We also significantly improved liquidity by approximately $51 million through reduced annualized operating costs, renegotiated collective bargaining agreements, employment cost reductions, and changes in operating practices. We also negotiated improvements through vendor/supplier programs by $40 million. We increased borrowing availability by $35 million through a new secured credit facility, and reduced interest on long-term debt for the next three years by $27 million. Despite all these so called "savings" the ship was still sinking. Outside the organization, Birmingham Steel of Birmingham, Alabama filed for Chapter-11 bankruptcy with a possible deal pending with Nucor Steel.

July and August were fairly decent months with regard to business upswing. We seemed to be making some progress on meeting our monthly business objectives. In fact, the outlook was promising enough for Weirton to announce the possibility of adding more employees.

The end of August we received disturbing news of another quarterly loss. Weirton reported losing $35.8 million for the second quarter. To date $80.4 million was lost for the first six months of the year, compared to $139.1 million for the same period last year. This was $58.7 million better than 2001 performance, but we were still losing money.

On August 16, Cold Metal Products of Youngstown, Ohio filed for Chapter-11 bankruptcy. But behind the scene, Mr. Wilbur L. Ross was continuing his quest of acquiring bankrupt steel companies and turning them into real tangible assets. He entered into agreement to purchase Acme Steel, and by the end of September a bankruptcy court approved the transaction.

September gave signs that the steel industry was continuing to sink deeper into a dark abyss where bankruptcies had already consumed 38 steel companies. Wheeling-Pittsburgh Steel was in the process of making plans to apply for the Byrd Bill (steel loan guarantee). If approved, it would use the assets to begin the process of coming out of bankruptcy.

Weirton was about ready to make some major announcements regarding changes to the corporate by-laws of the company. These "proposed charter changes" [2] had been discussed for a couple of months and were now ready to be made public. The main reason was Weirton did not have sufficient capital or internal funds to pursue an acquisition strategy, especially if something promising came along. Under current distressed industry conditions, Weirton believed that there might be opportunities to purchase steel assets on acceptable terms in the near future. Success in making acquisitions, however, would require the infusion of substantial equity or an equity-like investment of anywhere between $50 - $100 million, depending on the type of acquisition. Given the company's diminished market value, the company must be prepared to issue equity securities to attract new investors that would allow those new investors to obtain a controlling interest in Weirton as part of a strategic acquisition. Although ownership interest of the current stockholders would decrease as a result of a large equity investment, Weirton believed that an acquisition coupled with a new investment would afford the opportunity to increase the economic value of the shares held by the current stockholders.

A couple of things needed to take place; such as removing, from the charter, language regarding "restrictive supermajority" and other voting provisions; insertion of terms regarding a "transformative event"; reducing the size of the board; and finally, increasing the authorized number of shares of Preferred and Common Stock. [2]

Failure of the stockholders to approve the charter proposals, especially with respect to acquisitions, and the ability of the company to obtain necessary acquisition funding would deny the company the opportunity to pursue its independent growth strategy, and render it more vulnerable to a future downturn in the steel industry business cycle. The other proposed changes to the board were minor in comparison. The company believed that in an industry downturn, similar to that experienced in 2000 and 2001, the company might be forced to seek bankruptcy protection or commence liquidation proceedings if these changes were not approved.

What the employees and stockholders didn't know was that behind the scenes work was nearing completion for the possible merger with Wheeling-Pittsburgh Steel. We were also in discussions with Wheeling-Pittsburgh Steel on the possible acquisition of their Ohio Coatings tin facility. But this information had to remain behind closed doors for obvious reasons. If any word would have leaked out it could have undermined our efforts. Rumors and speculations was something we didn't want started.

September was going to be a very busy month. We needed to get the word out about the changes to the charter and communicate exactly what all the changes meant to all employees and shareholders. So the next two months would be a true test of our ability to communicate the information for a positive result. The biggest hurdle was to get the correct information out to every person, so that ever person clearly understood the meaning. People would twist and turn the information, sometimes for their own self-fulfillment, and then the information would be wrong. As more incorrect and twisted information got out the more confused individuals became. We needed some communications vehicle to provide consistent and accurate information about the proxy vote.

Weirton held numerous internal and external meetings to make sure employees and shareholders had an opportunity to ask questions and receive consistent and concise answers. This would probably be the biggest decision shareholders would make since the original vote for the ESOP. Phone banks were set up in the basement of the General Office and volunteers were asked to take turns during daylight hours, and not only call shareholders, but have shareholders call in to have someone provide answers to their questions. This process would continue right up to the deadline for the votes to be counted.

It was announced by Wheeling-Pittsburgh Steel that they were in the process of applying for the steel loan guarantee for the entire $250 million amount. Approval would provide the opportunity for them to emerge from bankruptcy.

By mid-September Geneva Steel of Vineyard, Utah announced it had filed for Chapter-11 bankruptcy. Then in early November, Weirton reported a $12.7 million loss for the third quarter. It was looking as though the company as a whole was really trying to improve not only operationally but stepping-up to achieve as many strategic objectives as possible to help stabilize the company's bottom line.

For the balance of November and into the month of December, a full-court press would have to take place to get the information for the proxy vote to all employees and shareholders. In addition, preparations were feverishly being made for putting together all the elements for the 2003 Business Plan, and have it ready for a December 11 Board of Directors meeting.

December's board of directors meeting would be different than previous years. Usually the board would only meet once a month but this was a special case and under special circumstances. The board would meet twice; once on Wednesday, December 11 with the full compliment of board members and again prior to the 6:00 p.m. annual stockholders meeting. The newly-appointed smaller board would then meet on Thursday, December 12 at 8:00 a.m., to review and approve the 2003 business plan and objectives.

During the course of the year, I had been placed on the distribution list for receiving copies of the company's financial information that also went out to all the board members. I was asked to question anything that didn't make sense to me. The reason for this assignment was for me to develop more of a financial awareness, and what trends I should be acutely aware of. Finance was always challenging for me, so by reviewing the financial information and asking questions, I could develop a better understanding of what the key indicators represented, and how they were interpreted to determine the health of the company. I was most appreciative of the Chief Financial Officer Mark Kaplan allowing me to be involved with this process. This process started early in the year and now, by the end of the year, I was able to ask what I considered to be intelligent questions.

On Monday, December 9, a meeting was held in the General Office boardroom as a dry run for the Wednesday board meeting. The meeting was chaired by the company controller and had representatives from all the key departments; sales, operations, finance, planning, and IT. The meeting reviewed all the data that would be presented to the board and insured that the information would be in fact accurately represented. The normal presentation media was a Microsoft PowerPoint presentation so that all attendees could see first hand the information and ask appropriate questions. The controller would note any changes or make any adjustments necessary on his hard copy before the slides were changed and prepared in final form for the board meeting in two days.

The most significant and most obvious problem, to me anyway, was the fact the business plan represented Weirton losing over $40 million in 2003. Not one department injected any comments about the projected loss. It just appeared this was the plan and this plan should just be accepted by the board. It was this "business as usual" attitude, right up to the end, with no one doing what was right for the company. *In this case an alarm had gone off, but no one else heard it.*

When the meeting was almost complete, the controller asked if there were any questions. I asked why we were about to present a negative business plan to the board without one alternative for improving the plan? One would have thought I had just told the world's funniest joke, for all the laughter. Operations said that I didn't understand how the plant floor operating units had to operate, and that they hoped they could get what they're projecting, and if they didn't; "oh well." Likewise, the sales group indicated I didn't understand that was all they could sell; markets were bad, so that's all you can do; "oh well." My only comment was, to the group as a whole, that if I was a member of the board of directors, there would no way in hell I would approve this plan. The meeting adjourned with shaking heads and more laughter. *Oh well!*

I turned to the controller and asked why no one came up with a contingency plan for turning around the negative numbers, and he said that he didn't know. I can only suspect that a possible reason was that too much work would have to be done trying to look for solutions to turn the negative numbers around. There might have been the realization that people might be placed in harms way and be held accountable for something. You need to sometimes keep a low profile or else you just might have to do some "real" work. However, as I look back on how the company actually operated, one could do just about anything, and still keep a job. There definitely wasn't much emphasis on accountability or performance, because if there was, I wouldn't be writing this book.

I had initially thought that the controller, after my comments, would have gone to the CFO and explained that the business plan contained no plan to turn around the negative numbers, but that apparently didn't happen. I guess I should have taken the initiative to follow-up with the CFO since he was the person to whom I reported, but that didn't happen either.

As for the board meeting on Wednesday, December 11, I was asked to attend mostly for my knowledge of the capital plan that would be presented for approval. If there were any specific questions regarding why certain IT items were necessary, I could provide the reasoning. This board consisted of all the existing board members and included Mr. Wendell W. Wood who would be the newest member to the board along with Mr. Mark E. Kaplan, my direct report.

Mr. Wendell W. Wood was President and Chairman of United Land Corporation and Weirton Steel's largest stockholder, owning some 4.9 million shares. Mr. Mark E. Kaplan was Senior Vice President of Finance and Administration, and Chief Financial Officer (CFO) of the corporation.

As the meeting began I could feel a lack of seriousness and interest, since for some it was their last meeting, and for others, tomorrow represented more of the formal, let's get down to business meeting. However, there was still a sense of deep understanding that the vote tonight, and what was being presented, could represent the final days for Weirton Steel.

Mr. Wendell Wood was the first to remark that the business plan represented only the negative side of the business with nothing regarding how the business could correct some of the shortcomings. He commented that the business plan represented over $40 million in losses and nothing to indicate alternatives to reduce those losses. Others in the meeting assured him that all of the issues would be addressed in detail at tomorrow's meeting.

On a more serious side, one slide in particular was most disturbing and alarming. It was an indicator of the health of the company. It was a slide showing how much liquidity the company projected over the course of 2003. Liquidity is the degree of ease and certainty of value with which a security can be converted into cash. It is the ability of a business to meet its obligations as they come due; the more liquid a business is, the better it is able to meet short-term financial obligations. The slide showed a significant drop between the end of March and the first of May. The liquidity would drop from an average $35 million to under $9 million during those months. If this number dropped further, or during this period some unexpected event occurred that would require immediate cash, the company would definitely have to file Chapter-11 bankruptcy. [3]

And so the meeting finally came to a close. It was almost an uneventful meeting, with only a couple of exceptions, and everyone gathered to say their goodbyes, even though they would be together at the stockholder meeting in just a few short hours.

The Annual Meeting of Stockholders of Weirton Steel Corporation came to order on Wednesday, December 11, 2002 at 6:00 p.m., at the Serbian-American Cultural Center in Weirton, West Virginia. The place was packed with standing-room only. This was the big event, the outcome that could give promise or demise to future events of Weirton Steel. Every one of us who had spent so many hours, especially behind the scenes, for so many months was finally here, and our questions would be answered. Did the majority of stockholders approve the proxy changes and the rest of the items on the agenda?

The required number of votes needed was 43 million votes. Unfortunately only 34 million votes were voted in favor of the changes. The proxy vote to change the corporate charter was defeated. My heart left my chest and went into my stomach, and my head felt like I had just recovered from a really bad hangover, dizzy and lightheaded. I just couldn't believe that after all the hard work by so many people that we came up nine million votes short. I said a prayer and asked the Lord for strengthen and guidance. We were going to need all the help we could get in the upcoming months.

The stockholders did however approve reducing the board members from 14 to 9, adding two new directors, Mr. Wood and Mr. Kaplan, along with some other changes that were requested. Serving for the last time were Mr. George Doty, Mr. D. Leonard Wise, Mr. Robert Reitman, Mr. Ralph Reins, and Mr. Dick Schubert. [4)]

I was privileged to work with some of the board members during my career: some up close and personal, while others just to recognize and say hello. They came from varied backgrounds, and had multiple years of experience in different areas of business. What I found remarkable was that the majority of board members were limited in knowledge of the steel industry with the exception of Mr. D. Leonard Wise. The make up of Weirton's board had been that way since the inception of ESOP: board members with no steel experience, only lawyers and consultants.

In my opinion and personal observations of Leonard Wise, I think he should have been named chairman of the board long before becoming a board member. He possessed a long list of tremendous attributes. The one attribute none of the others had that he possessed was common sense, along with a warehouse of knowledge unsurpassed by anyone that I've come in contact with in the steel business. The only exception might be our first chairman Mr. Robert Loughhead. Mr. Loughhead never survived long enough to realize any of his desired goals and that represented a significant loss to Weirton Steel. We will never know what Weirton could have become under his leadership. Little did I realize that the admiration that I had felt for Len would soon develop into a very personal working relationship. This was a relationship that would test our utmost abilities.

The next morning Thursday, December 12, at 7:00 a.m., I arrived at the General Office and headed to the boardroom. One of my tasks was to make sure all of the audio/visual equipment was functioning properly before each board meeting, and to load the presentation software onto the computer to make sure it displayed correctly. After I touched base with Mark Kaplan to make sure he was satisfied, I quietly left and would only respond if there was a problem, which didn't happen very often.

Usually, the board meeting was over around noon or slightly after. I anxiously waited until about 3:00 p.m., to phone Mark Kaplan to inquire how the board meeting went. However, I was disappointed that even after several attempts throughout the remainder of the afternoon Mark didn't return any of my repeated phone attempts.

The next morning, Friday, December 13, I arrived at my office about 7:45 a.m., and was presented with a flashing red light on my phone. This was an indication that I had a voice mail message. When I listened to the message it was from John Walker's secretary informing me of a meeting in the boardroom at 8:15 a.m., and I needed to attend. It was urgent!

When I arrived I knew something was about to be announced because all the department heads started filing in. I took my seat next to the controller and asked him if he knew what the meeting was all about, and he said he heard the board meeting didn't go very well, and John Walker would probably let us know what happened.

With almost all the executives present, Mark Kaplan entered the room but John Walker was nowhere in sight. As Mark started the meeting he said something like, "since I'm not sure just how to say this, I'm just going to say that in yesterday's board meeting John got his ass kicked up between his shoulder blades." He stated that there was no way the board was going to accept a negative business plan for 2003. I suddenly turned to look at the controller as he turned toward me. Mark caught glimpses of the movement and asked what was going on. The controller then informed Mark that on Monday during the dry run I had brought up that same exact remark. Mark then told everyone present to be in the boardroom on Monday at 8:00 a.m. stating that John Walker wanted everyone present to "kick-off" charting a new course and direction for the corporation. [5]

On Monday, December 16, John Walker started the meeting by stating that management and union together had to find multiple ways to lower costs so we could keep cash flowing. We needed to do it quickly. John turned to me and asked me to try and uncover as much information about this new ISG Company whose strategy was to buy up all of the bankrupt steel assets, and find out about their business model and strategy and how their plan was able to work. He wanted to know how they were able to operate with so few people and still manage to produce a significant volume of steel. The company, International Steel Group, (ISG) was currently operating LTV and Acme Steel companies. It was in negotiations with bankrupt Bethlehem Steel. *This was not going to be an easy task, but I had to try.*

John outlined what he considered a five-step plan, with cost reductions in five specific areas that, if satisfactorily reached, would sustain us and would allow us to reverse the 2003 business plan to generate positive cash flow. It would keep Weirton as a viable corporation, hopefully until a recovery or upswing of the market would happen. Those five areas were commercial (sales), purchasing (raw materials), human resources (pension benefits and labor), operations (yield, production and manpower), and finance (SG&A or selling, general and administrative expenses). The total plan was expected to save $100 million. 6) *Here we go again.*

The five-step plan was a way to reverse the 2003 Business Plan for a positive outcome, improve (increase) liquidity, create cost saving initiatives in five specific areas, modify the labor agreement, and improve our senior credit facility. This was all to be completed by March 1. *Talk about pulling rabbits out of your hat.*

It was also announced that Wheeling-Pittsburgh Steel was ready to file a new plan of reorganization from bankruptcy. It was also announced the PBGC or (Pension Benefit Guarantee Corporation) was taking over the pension plan for more than 35,000 workers and retirees from National Steel Corporation.

I was having a really difficult time deciding how to get started on getting information about ISG. It was going to be a very difficult task of trying to assimilate data and information about ISG when they had only begun doing business a few short months earlier. There wasn't even information on the Internet yet to try and reference. I started with our director of corporate development and strategy to sort of kick-start the process. He was only able to get bits and pieces from his steel contacts and other counterparts.

From the little information he was able to provide, I found that a company out of Pittsburgh was actually providing the information technology support for ISG, and was using a new kind of "out-of-the-box" software package. They also had somehow provided back-office (financial, human resources, payroll, etc.) support to ISG, and I needed to understand who this company was and whether they were willing to or could help Weirton.

I placed a series of phone calls to this company in Pittsburgh called Hudson Global Resources. Hudson Global Resources was a division of the Hudson Highland Group that employed some 4000 people in 27 countries. Hudson Global Resources helped clients throughout the employment lifecycle by providing a company with specialized professional staffing, outsourcing, and human resource consulting and inclusion solutions.

As mentioned earlier, ISG was able to buy bankrupt steel assets for pennies on the dollar. It didn't have to worry about employees, retirees, pension plans, health care, life insurance or the hourly cost of doing business. It had in its power the ability to set the mark for each of these costly legacy items that other companies struggled to fund. The one anchor-weight around the neck of most business entities, and the straw that brings them to their knees, is the inability to fund the promises to workers that were made some 30 or more years ago. These "defined" plans are just too costly to fund. Companies just can't afford the old ways of doing business if they want not only to remain competitive in a global arena, but be successful and grow.

ISG was able not only to avoid these pitfalls but to reshape the way steel was being made. Taking these "legacy" costs out of the equation allowed ISG to run leaner, and provide a means of making money at the same time. The major advantage ISG now had over their competition was they could develop new work rules with union employees. This gave the upper hand to the company. Not only did they set new work rule regulations, but also were able to hand select the workforce through drug screening and hair sampling for DNA evidence of drug use. *Boy, that's really something!*

Hudson Global Resources won a bid contract for supplying ISG with information technology services including providing resources for much of their back office functions. Hudson Global convinced ISG to invest in a new "out-of-the-box" technology called Axiom® Software developed by a company called Axis Computer Systems Incorporated. Axis Computer Systems was at that time the leading supplier of enterprise management systems software for the metals, wire and cable industries, and was headquartered in Marlborough, Massachusetts. Their product termed Axiom® was a family of application software products tightly integrated so they worked seamlessly. They replaced the antiquated nonintegrated system software of the steel industry that was developed in house. The type of software applications currently being run in the steel industry could be compared to silos. Each silo represented a different application and the silos were not connected together. If you were required to make even a simple change to the software application, you had to make changes, sometimes to hundreds of software applications and often with disastrous results. So changes were often frowned upon.

However, this new Axis Computer System software was designed to run, as is, right out of the box. Changes to the software, although sometimes required, were not recommended but could be made. Even if changes were made, that one change would automatically change all the other programs it was associated with. So modifications could be made without worry that some other part of the system would be adversely affected.

I began by inviting the Hudson senior account executive for technology to come down to Weirton so we could begin to explore some ideas of compressing not only the computer systems within Weirton, but also to reduce the workforce similar to that of ISG. I wanted to see what the overall cost savings would generate.

Chapter Six – The Year was 2003

In early January, we learned that ISG would begin proceedings to purchase bankrupt Bethlehem Steel Corporation. These guys were really starting to move and move quickly. As quickly as they purchased a company, they started putting the assets into production, making steel and making steel at a lower cost. *They were making money!*

We had a series of back-to-back meetings with the Hudson Group trying to understand the ISG concept. It took probably six or more meetings of trying to understand their ideas. The primary reason was the Hudson Group was under a confidentiality agreement not to discuss any of the details of the ISG contract.

So, my tactic was to have the Hudson Group set up a similar, but not exact, structure for Weirton Steel as they did for the ISG group. Given our employee numbers, departments, and the like, I was able to extrapolate what I needed to begin to make Weirton look like ISG, without legal ramification toward the Hudson Group or without knowing what ISG actually looked like from the inside of their plants.

We essentially looked at two distinct scenarios: one scenario included making all the physical changes to Weirton while keeping the existing computer network of applications. The other scenario was making the physical change to Weirton while moving to the Axis computer system software. (The physical changes at Weirton would reduce or cut back on manpower across all departments to scale down employees similar to what ISG had done.)

As a sidebar to everything else going on, I was still in the process of negotiating with Wheeling-Pittsburgh Steel on a merger with Weirton. I was probably a few weeks shy of having the financial information complete on how the two companies could merge their respective IT departments so that neither company would lose a dollar of revenue or a ton of steel. This information was critical, as it would be used to secure funding so Weirton Steel could buy the assets of Wheeling-Pittsburgh Steel.

Throughout the month of January, we held at least one if not more strategy meetings per week with a select group of management personnel from the IT Department. These sessions kept everyone on the same page, and allowed us to discuss any potential problems that might have surfaced since our last meeting. This group was also prepared to work with their respective counterpart from Wheeling–Pittsburgh Steel.

In early February, management and union had reached a tentative union agreement. The current contract expired in March 2004. It was noted that expected savings from the new agreement could reach $40 million dollars. Even though wage adjustments were made for all employees, there were changes made to vacation pay and the health care plan, as well as providing the ISU with a greater role in future discussions concerning the viability and operational aspects of the company.

About this time, I received some really good news from our Hudson consultants: they were able to release to me certain manpower numbers of the various departments being operated at ISG. They were no longer tied to a confidentiality agreement at least in certain parts. This was a huge help for me in setting up the statistical models I had been preparing. These models were used in our management reviews as we tried to understand exactly what we could do, and what the impact was going to be. We were just about ready to make a management presentation to show the impact of what the Axis computer software could do for Weirton Steel.

This was truly the break I was looking for. With this new information I was able to really fine tune our strategic model and begin holding weekly strategy meetings with senior management. It made the models more realistic in terms of people and costs to operate the company. These meetings would allow us to formulate a strategy that was similar in design to that of ISG. The only exception was Weirton would still be responsible for the legacy costs of retirees, pension plan and health insurance. So in order to try to meet everything in the middle of the road, I was proposing additional manpower cuts to help offset our legacy costs.

We received more bad news as Weirton reported a $24.3 million quarterly loss. Additionally, Wheeling-Pittsburgh Steel received word that their application for a $250 million Steel Loan Guarantee was rejected, serving another powerful blow to Wheeling-Pitt; however, I saw this as good news for Weirton. This made the merger that much more attractive and doable and that much more important to resolve.

In March, word had gotten out that Weirton and Wheeling-Pitt were once again talking about a merger. These meetings were getting more intense since the rejection of the Steel Loan application. Wheeling-Pitt's pension plan was terminated and taken over by the PBGC. That turn of events was not going to keep Wheeling-Pitt down and they made a new loan application and resubmitted it to the Steel Loan Guarantee committee to consider. This application encompassed the installation of an electric arc furnace; with some luck it might get approved.

Weirton on the other hand was continuing to struggle with cost-saving programs that truly would impact the bottom line in a positive way if we could only succeed in delivering these goals. We were making progress, but unfortunately not fast enough. We were asking all employees for concessions to lower our health care costs. This was going to be a struggle, not for the salaried employees, but for the union employees because it would have to be approved by the membership.

John Walker and Mark Kaplan made a series of trips to Washington, D. C. to rally support for the merger. Meetings were to take place with members of Senator Byrd and Rockefeller's office and the office of Congressman Alan Mollohan. We needed everyone to know that the merger was in fact ready to move forward. We just needed the Steel Loan Board to DENY Wheeling-Pitt's application. Since they were denied on their original application in February it would be just as easy to deny their newest application. If the application for the loan were approved, then the entire deal would be over. We would never know what combining both companies could have been accomplished.

The Emergency Steel Loan Guarantee Board was comprised of three (3) members from three (3) separate departments. The board consisted of the Chairman of the Board of Governors of the Federal Reserve System, who acted as the Chairman of the Steel Board; the Chairman of the Securities and Exchange Commission, and the Secretary of Commerce.

The only thing any of our elected officials had to do was personally discuss the situation with one or more of the board members to explain that a deal had been tentatively reached, and by denying the loan the deal could proceed to the next level. If there was any doubt in their mind about approving the loan, rejecting it would work in both companies' favor. It was not suggested that anyone do anything illegal, but provide only the facts for a better decision to be rendered. If in the end the board did approve the loan, then the board did in fact make the correct decision.

On the financial side, Mark Kaplan had some great success putting together a financial package to make the merger work. He had secured financing from four banking institutions from New York totaling $500 million, twice the amount of the steel loan. In order for this to take place, Weirton had to secure those loans with some of our own money; several million dollars of our own money.

The stage was nearly set. Some very involved meetings were taking place between senior management officials from Weirton and Wheeling-Pitt. These meetings were held with Weirton Steel and Wheeling-Pittsburgh Steel executives to discuss the specifics of the merger. Although I was not in attendance at any of these private meetings, word had it that there were disagreements on how the actual merger would take place. Weirton would be the controlling company, but who would be president? Since Weirton had an independent union and the United Steelworkers of America represented Wheeling-Pitt, how would that combination work? Just how many people would lose their jobs? What type of production would be separated out? What about the infamous electric arc furnace, do we put it in or leave it out? There were arguments on both sides for and against the installation of the furnace. Most of the minor issues could have been worked out to everyone's satisfaction after the merger took place. *I guess we will never know that outcome either.*

On March 24 and March 25, I met with the Executive Vice President and Chief Finance Officer from Wheeling-Pitt, to describe and discuss our strategy on how the two companies were planning to merge their respective IT departments. This was probably one of the most critical tasks because Weirton's systems were fairly new, but Wheeling-Pitt's were quite old and antiquated. We were just going to transfer as much information electronically, keeping both companies separated in the computer, but combine revenues and steel production. A point in time would be decided when all of Wheeling-Pitt's systems would be shut down, and Weirton's systems would run everything. This could only occur once the data was totally transferred to the Weirton system.

After our last meeting on March 25, the CFO stated he really thought we had everything nailed down, and he really didn't see anything out of the ordinary. I'll never forget his parting words: "Tom, despite all the hard work everyone has put into this, you do realize that if our loan is approved, all bets are off."

After the meetings and in the days that followed, I kept Mark Kaplan and John Walker abreast of my activities and stated that everything was ready to go. I asked what the odds were of the loan being denied. John stated that his sources in Washington indicated that the loan would not be granted.

Then at roughly 6:35 p.m., on March 27, a local news channel broke the story that Wheeling-Pitt had received approval for the $250 million Emergency Steel Loan and would begin the process of coming out of bankruptcy. This was another really bad day for Weirton.

In February and March, we conducted special weekly meetings, together with senior management, to focus on our revenue and liquidity side of the business. It kept appearing that no matter what was being done our liquidity kept slipping. If this trend continued, we might not be able to make it past May. *We just couldn't succeed in accomplishing our goals.*

The union appeared to want to help though a series of cost-saving initiatives. So far they had ratified a new contract that represented wage concessions, a pension freeze and elimination of a scheduled $1 an hour pay raise. They also made a provision not to receive their vacation pay all at one time, but to leverage it when their seniority date occurred. That way the money was allocated throughout the year instead of having the company upfront everything at one time. Mark Glyptis indicated about $38 million in savings would be realized.

More management strategy meetings were being held to keep a running tab of what was happening on a weekly basis. Vendor meetings proved to be very beneficial in helping to reduce costs. We looked at all types of outsourcing solutions, but none of them provided any immediate relief to our plight.

It was announced that National Steel's assets that were being purchased by U.S. Steel were finally approved. *Boy, how time changes everything.*

Weirton management continued to talk about changing the health care costs with not only employees but retirees as well. The union however, did not find a need to join in the program. They felt that the savings realized from the union contract was enough. However, the retirees were really having a hard time understanding all the changes, and then some of the presentations being conducted didn't send out the same message. It was an ongoing challenge to try and keep the message consistent because many of our former retirees really didn't grasp or fully understand the situation that was playing out.

More meetings were being held, now daily, to review the liquidity of the company and to gauge exactly where we stood. In addition to looking at liquidity, we also looked to the horizon to determine if we could predict with any degree of certainty, how much longer pricing and the market was going to be in the tank. In one of the meetings it was decided that Weirton should make an application to the Steel Loan Board. It surely couldn't hurt. *But, in the back of my mind, I knew we had waited entirely too long.*

We received some positive news regarding the health care response from the retirees. All the meetings held with numerous groups of retirees had paid off. Weirton would net about $10 million in savings.

However, as the week of May 12 though the 16 came and went, it was, in my mind at least, the inevitable feeling that we just couldn't hold on for much longer. We had a couple of very large payments overdue, and the vendors were putting pressure on us to pay. We were reminded about the nervousness of the vendors in our daily meetings but just kept trying not to dwell on them and to concentrate on increasing revenue.

Then on Monday, May 19, to everyone's shock and amazement, **Weirton Steel Corporation filed for Chapter-11 bankruptcy protection.** Company spokesperson Greg Warren, stated that the bankruptcy could not wait another day. If we tried to push past May into June, the company would probably have to file Chapter 7 and liquidate all the assets. What a truly sad day for Weirton Steel, the community, all the employees, and the retirees. Those like my father would never believe this day would or could ever come. The ISU and Mark Glyptis of course were very vocal about the filing and criticized management and especially John Walker for allowing this to happen. But, Mark knew exactly how this happened; he was privileged, especially as a board member, to the same information we all had. If fact, Mark, as a member of the Finance and Strategic Planning Committee should have foreseen this coming.

A series of meetings had to be held with all our employees and vendors to explain what was next in this process. I didn't even know what was happening, so how was I going to explain what was happening. Those were truly troubling meetings because everyone, employees and contractors alike, were always looking for a positive answer to their questions, and I couldn't give them one.

Then to make matters even worse Weirton, at the end of May, announced a quarterly loss of $74.8 million. Weirton had lost more than $700 million in the last two years alone.

In June, the floodgates opened, and I can't tell you how many attorneys and legal people came in. We contracted at $150,000/month an advisory fee to Houlihan, Lockey, Howard and Zuklin Capital of Los Angeles, California. *These legal people were everywhere.*

As of February 28, 2003, Weirton had an under-funded pension obligation of $435 million. It would require nearly $70 million per year from 2003 through 2007 to meet the minimum funding obligation, or a total of $350 million. So the PBGC was named to the Unsecured Creditor Committee. *Weirton had no intention of contributing one cent to the plan; how sad for the hundreds of employees counting on their pensions to be secure.*

John Walker announced that another round of management layoffs would happen and the five percent wage cuts we took earlier in the year would still be in effect. However, on the positive side Mark Kaplan was successful in receiving $225 million in DIP financing from Fleet Capital Group, Chicago. (*Debtor-in-possession (DIP) financing is a special form of financing provided for companies in financial distress or under the Chapter-11 bankruptcy process. Usually, this security is more senior than other debt, equity, or any other securities issued by a company. It gives a troubled company a new start, albeit under stricter conditions.*)

We also made an application to the Emergency Steel Loan Guarantee Board for $175 million to help assist with Chapter-11 reorganization. The Byrd Bill at this point in time had been facing opposition from a number of individuals in Washington and no one knew how long it would be available.

On June 27, we learned that John Walker had resigned his position as CEO of Weirton Steel. It looked like John had his interests and not those of the company at heart to make such a quick departure.

He really didn't accomplish that much since taking office, and he surely didn't make any of the management changes I had hoped for.

June also saw Wheeling-Pitt getting approval for their reorganization plan to emerge from bankruptcy. The month of July began with the union negotiating a new contract and the beginning of management layoffs.

All the work done in the previous six months was essentially down the drain. The attorneys and their legal teams were hard at work trying to understand everything we did, how we did it, who the vendors were, what they did and what we could do without. The biggest task of all was to understand how much money Weirton owed to our vendor community. You have to remember, when bankruptcy is imminent you start by not paying your bills in order to save cash to prevent filing for as long as possible. *Now we have to pay the piper.*

With everything "slip-sliding" for the last several months, I slightly took my eye off the Hudson Group and all the outsourcing initiatives we were exploring. So, in between legal meetings, with multitudes of attorneys, I was able to once again concentrate on putting the ISG model together for Weirton. I sat with Mark Kaplan on several occasions to discuss what I was doing and told him this might be our only hope. Mark had an enormous task of trying to keep our heads above water. His task was like trying to change a flat tire on a car doing 80 miles per hour.

Weirton, again, reported a loss of $44 million for the second quarter of 2003. Wheeling-Pitt's re-organization plan was approved for them to move out of bankruptcy and only several weeks later it announced they had formally exited from Chapter-11 bankruptcy.

We finished the month of July and started the month of August with a series of very late management meetings. We were reviewing the data that I had compiled about how ISG was able to do what they were doing. These back and forth meetings were intended to look at all the possible data about how each department operated and determine whether Weirton could operate in a similar fashion.

Then on August 6, Weirton announced our new leadership. Mr. D. Leonard Wise would become our CEO, and Mark E. Kaplan would become our President and CFO. What a roller coaster ride for Mark.

What I began to witness was the unwillingness of several departments to even come to the table and discuss any "change the corporation" options. Len stated that everyone needed to look at my data, discuss the options, and be prepared to make a decision that would benefit the corporation. This was not the time to put our tail between our legs, so to speak. So, the meetings continued nearly everyday and into the weekend of August 7 and 8, a Saturday and Sunday. When we finished, we had decided unanimously on a document that, once the data was re-verified, would be ready to present to the union leadership.

  That week represented a great deal of work for me. With the help of the Hudson Group, who verified our data and confirmed that our approach to downsize Weirton Steel similar to what ISG was doing was very realistic. We developed two scenarios: a moderate approach and a radical approach. By mid-week, we abandoned the radical approach so as not to scare off the union. We could always bring that scenario up at a later time.

  However, on the cusp of the leadership announcement, there was mention of retention bonuses for Len and Mark. Mark would receive $1.4 million and Len would receive $1.35 million. There was also $4 million going to nine unidentified management personnel. *(For those interested, I was not part of the nine management personnel. Darn!)* As one would imagine, the union officials were up in arms. Simultaneously, it was announced that our current structured loan agreements would be in default if John Walker or Mark Kaplan were not in a command leadership role at Weirton. This was cited in section 10, page 62 of the 200-page DIP financing legal agreement between Weirton and the Lenders. The company would stand in default of its loan obligation due to "the failure of one of John Walker or Mark Kaplan to function as chief executive officer of borrower (WS), unless replaced within 10 days thereafter with a chief executive officer or chief restructuring officer acceptable to agent (lender) or with majority lender…." Since John had already left, that put Mark in the driver's seat.

  Later on August 8, Attorney Mark Freedlander would argue in U.S. Bankruptcy Court for the retention bonuses. Judge E. Edward Friend granted not only the bonuses but the appointments of Wise and Kaplan. This of course did not sit well with the union and we believe it represented the one reason they ignored our proposal and decided to negotiate their own deal.

On Friday, August 15, the majority of the management team, along with members of the union executive committee and Mark Glyptis, met in the boardroom and presented the proposal to the union to moderately alter the way we would operate as a corporation going forward. Every department within Weirton would be downsized, with some departments consolidated. We needed to reduce the salary, salary non-exempt, and union work force to a number that would mirror what ISG was doing. After deliberating nearly all afternoon and answering numerous questions, Mark Glyptis and his senior leaders left the room. In summary, the union wanted to look at two scenarios: one as a stand-alone restructured company, and the other if the company was sold. I could tell he didn't particularly care for either proposal. But, the stand-alone proposal was going to be very similar to what the union ultimately accepted when ISG bought the company. After the meeting was over, the union indicated it would review the information and get back to executive management. We never did hear from them regarding the proposal, even after repeated attempts to set follow-up meetings.

We later learned that Mark Glyptis and several key union members were in fact talking with key ISG senior management including Mr. Wilbur L. Ross himself. I don't know with any degree of certainty, but I believe they used the information, along with the document we gave them and used both of them to work with ISG. They ultimately won the deal.

Weirton also announced that in July, it missed a $20 million pension payment, and the company stated it notify the PBGC of the missed payment. As previously stated, Weirton had an under-funded pension plan in the sum of $435 million as of February 28, 2003. Court documents indicate the company was required to pay no less than $70 million in contributions, per year, in years 2003 through 2007 to meet the minimum funding requirements. As of March 2003 Weirton had an estimated accrued liability for other post-retirement benefits of approximately $335 million, with an actual annual cash cost of no less than $30 million per year. This was not good.

The union had been busy recruiting a new member to represent their interest on the board of directors. They recruited Mr. Ted Arneault, President and CEO of nearby Mountaineer Race Track and Gaming Resort as their representative. Although I didn't know Mr. Arneault personally, I did see the results of his efforts at Mountaineer, which were amazing. He was an idea and results oriented individual, and probably one of the best selections the union could have made.

That same week Weirton submitted a $10 million grant request to the West Virginia Economic Development committee for funding for the Polymer Coating Technology we wanted to see become operational. However, the very next day Weirton Steel received notice that the project would not be considered for funding and our application was refused.

By the end of August Weirton posted another $14.8 million loss. Weirton's company spokes person stated that there were other companies looking at the possibility of acquiring Weirton, including ISG.

Weirton Steel and the union were now engaged in very difficult negotiating sessions for a new contract. On August 27, ISG Chief Finance Officer Mr. Len Anthony and other key ISG officials toured the Weirton Steel facilities.

The month of September was full of very awkward weeks. Weirton made and approved several modifications to save the company nearly $350 million dollars and was looking for ways to help fund the pension plan. But, with everything else going on, Weirton was focused on just keeping the blast furnaces operational, while negotiations continued with the union for new contract language.

Weirton realized in early September that trying to get everything ready to get out of bankruptcy by September 16 was an impossible task. So Weirton applied and received a three-month extension moving the date to December 15.

On October 8, Weirton Steel filed its plan of reorganization to emerge from bankruptcy as a stand-alone company and if approved would be a viable entity again by December 31. Terms were to have emergency financing guaranteed under the Emergency Steel Loan Guarantee program to the tune of $175 million. Chicago based Fleet Capital Corporation would provide $175 million, if the loan board approved the plan.

With ISG talking with our union officials, and to Mark Glyptis specifically, we were not sure what the outcome would be. However, Mark Glyptis did state that the Independent Steelworkers Union was in a strong position to determine the entire outcome of any reorganization plan because a new labor contract had to be in place before the court or creditors could sign off on anyone's plan. Mark Glyptis stated, "We are keeping our options open as we go down this dual path. We have not eliminated any potential options, and we will continue to keep our options open."

By mid-October, Weirton Steel asked the court to move forward with its workforce reduction program with the intent to save the company approximately $10 million annually. There really wasn't anything the company could do about the pension plan. It would just have to be taken over by the PBGC. And so on October 21, the PBGC assumed responsibility of the company's pension plan for 9200 workers and retirees. The plan, which now was only 39 percent funded with $530 million in assets to cover almost $1.35 billion in benefit liabilities was now in the hands of the PBGC. Of the $825 million in total underfunding, the PBGC estimated that it would be liable for about $697 million. If the PBGC didn't take over the plan at this point in time, it would run the risk of incurring additional losses of $147 million in shutdown benefits, a form of severance pay that companies do not set aside any money in advance to fund.

The very next day, October 18, the court approved the workforce reduction program. However, Mark Glyptis continued his campaign of being critical of executive management. He publicly stated he would not work one hour in the mill if Section 1113 of the U.S. Bankruptcy code was unilaterally implemented. Section 1113 would allow Weirton Steel to operate in bankruptcy without a labor agreement. *Nice to see union and management working together.*

Initiating the layoffs would cost between $4.5 and $6.8 million but would ultimately save $11.7 million annually. There would also be a reduction of 175 of the company's 472 management personnel.

In early November all the banks that had an interest in Weirton Steel filed objections to the company's disclosure statement and included the PBGC as well. Weirton hoped that the loan board would make their decision by mid-month.

On November 14, we received conditional approval of $145 million from the Emergency Steel Loan Board, but they rejected the $35 million earmarked to help build the Polymer Coating Line.

The union kept rejecting offers to come to the table and work through the proposed restructuring issues. Granted, we asked for some significant reductions but nothing different than if ISG would come in and negotiate a deal. We didn't want ISG coming in, maybe as a last resort, but certainly not now. We had a workable plan but needed union cooperation to make it a reality. Weirton's company spokesperson said, "We have asked the ISU to agree to significant reductions. We are hopeful they will respond positively. We have asked that they cut 450 employees." To that end the union never did respond.

The very next day, November 15, the Judge approved the Weirton Steel reorganization plan. Four days later we posted a $37.2 million loss for the third quarter. Weirton was also looking into the retirees having an opportunity to select alternative health care and life insurance programs.

Weirton proposed a new labor agreement to the ISU. The company stated it already agreed to a benefit package for the retirees that exceeded what had been given by competing steelmakers coming out of bankruptcy. The package included continuing levels of life insurance. However, the union wasn't or didn't seem very impressed.

It was so difficult for me, personally, to read a comment from our U.S. Senator Jay Rockefeller stating that he was in favor of steel consolidation. *Where was he six months ago? What effort did he personally put forth to help achieve that consolidation?* If the Senator and our other congressional leaders were aware of the need for consolidation why weren't they leading the charge? Why weren't they in the meeting with Weirton and Wheeling-Pitt? It was apparent to me they weren't looking out for the best interests of either company.

In early December Weirton announced additional layoffs of 85 employees, including 75 hourly and 10 management personnel. We were looking at getting another extension to complete the reorganization plan.

A LOOK BACK AT THE WAY WEIRTON WAS AND WHAT WEIRTON LOOKS LIKE TODAY!

In 1952 E.T. Weir stood as a very proud man. He had built his dream and was witness to its success. He could marvel at his greatest accomplishment, Weirton Steel.

The Mill Administration Building (MAB) stood as the first executive offices of Weirton Steel. Today the offices are for Mittal Steel – Weirton division employees.

In 1960 the executive offices moved from the MAB to a new building at the south end of Three Springs Drive. The General Office Building (GO) stood for nearly 50 years.

From 2008 through 2010 the GO was demolished. In its place a new Wal-Mart Super Store was built.

This 1956 photo showed men and women coming out of Gate #1. The picture shows hustling people on a busy North Main Street in Weirton.

This 2010 photo shows no men or women coming out of Gate #1 on North Main Street. The buildings are long gone and all that is left are "potholes," grass and weeds.

This 1950 photo was the "crossroads" into Weirton. It is the intersection of County Road – Pennsylvania Ave – Main Street. People lined the streets in celebration.

This 2010 photo stands without a marker to preserve the memory of the "crossroad." This intersection will never see celebration again in our foreseeable future.

Weirton Steel had four Blast Furnaces. From left to right are (No. 1, No. 2, No. 3). No. 4 is just to the right out of the picture. They are in full production making iron.

Today, 2010, all four blast furnaces are sitting idle, completely cold, and will never make iron again.

A site that most thought we would never see; the Independent Steelworkers Union hall, now in 2010, home to the United Steelworkers of America.

Another site most thought we would never see is the mammoth giant BOP, with two – 360 ton vessels, sitting idle, awaiting a torch to end steelmaking forever.

In 1984, thousands of men, women and children lined this street, as far as the eye could see, to get a first hand glimpse of our new steel leaders as they led the July 4 parade down Main Street. Hundreds more waved out of windows or stood on the roof tops.

Thousands of people had the hope that another 100 years of steelmaking was in their future.

White smoke (steam) could be seen rising from the enormous stacks of the BOP as a new era in steelmaking began.

This 2010 photo depicts the same street but a deserted town. Hundreds of people have left while those that stayed, pray, that a miracle might somehow happen. The giant BOP stacks still reach into the sky, silently standing guard over the community. The BOP waits its final demise; to be demolished with the rest of the mill.

The final chapter of Weirton Steel is nearly complete and so is over 100 years of steelmaking. A similar hill overlooks Weirton Steel, once a vibrant thriving steel mill, but something is drastically missing.

E.T. Weir is gone from this photo. This one mans dream and reality have faded. Sadly, the hopes and dreams of so many generations of steelmakers are gone as well. Bankrupt in 2003, International Steel Group (ISG) purchased assets in 2004; Mittal Steel purchased ISG in 2005, and shutdown steelmaking operations that same year.

Steelmaking in Weirton, West Virginia had come to a final end!

Chapter Seven – The year was 2004

In early January, there was absolutely no word about any possible deal with ISG to purchase Weirton Steel. Mr. Rodney Mott, CEO of ISG simply stated that, "There had been some preliminary discussion some time ago."

To make matters worse, there was a coke shortage that was affecting Weirton's production of hot metal at the blast furnace. As a result, Weirton needed to temporarily curtail certain operations. This led to some temporary layoffs. The temporary layoffs could exceed a month, affecting several hundred workers. It was estimated that 80 percent of our production had been halted. This coke shortage, in part, was from a fire in a West Virginia mine that supplied coal to U.S. Steel Corporation. We purchased the refined coal as coke from U.S. Steel. Our annual consumption of coke was roughly 1.2 million tons. However, because China was using the biggest supply of coke, there appeared to be a world-wide shortage. By mid-January, temporary layoffs at Weirton would reach nearly 800 workers due to the coke situation.

The union continued to be mum about negotiating with ISG. However, industry analyst's suspected that ISG was only interested in Weirton's tin plate. Steel analyst Chuck Bradford, from the Bradford Research/Soleil Securities in New York, indicated that "ISG was interested in tin only, and from the ISU standpoint, I wonder if they would be willing to accept a labor contract, similar to the old LTV and Bethlehem contract. That would wipe out all retiree's pensions or health care, leaving only whatever the PBGC would cover. The best I can tell, ISU had been unwilling to agree to anything like that with the management of Weirton." [1] Union President Mark Glyptis denied those claims.

As Weirton prepared for additional layoffs due to the nationwide coke shortage, Wheeling-Pitt emerged from bankruptcy. On January 29, U.S. Bankruptcy Court Judge E. Edward Friend extended the reorganization deadline for Weirton Steel to March 31.

As I mentioned earlier, the union, for whatever reason, was unwilling to engage in meaningful discussions, whether with contract negotiations or the restructuring of the company. In my opinion, this is what Mark Glyptis and the union had been waiting for all these years. What better position to be in the driver's seat! They could control their own destiny and get what they wanted. They didn't need Weirton management anymore. They were in control and they would decide their own future with someone new. It was reported that Mark Glyptis stated that he never met anyone as honest and trustworthy as Mr. Mott or Mr. Wilbur L. Ross, but only time would tell.

As the month of February started, Mark Glyptis decided to change tactics and announced that Weirton's management team was unwilling to engage in meaningful discussions. A new labor contract was paramount to emerge from bankruptcy. *Boy, is he positioning himself or what? Not wanting to negotiate! The company was asking the union nearly every week to sit down and discuss our proposal.*

Weirton made an announcement that vacation pay for all union employees, totaling $13 million, would not be paid out in the traditional lump sum process, but would be distributed when employees took their vacations.

Weirton also announced a $551.4 million loss in December. There was a one-time charge of $536.6 million by the PBGC when it took over the pension plan. Mark Kaplan stated that at the end of January, Weirton was not cash flow positive. He stated, "Things are looking better regarding our company's cash flow as a result of increased selling prices in the international steel market, however, the extraordinarily high cost of raw materials and the ongoing worldwide coke shortage continues to limit our incoming cash flow from sales." [2] *At this point in time, who cared?*

This was not good news. But there was good news about the opening of the Pineville, West Virginia coal mine. This production would help to reduce the coke shortage problem.

Then we received the news that we really didn't want to hear. On February 18, the International Steel Group (ISG) announced it would buy Weirton Steel pending approval of the court. This deal was worth $225 million dollars. They would acquire all of Weirton's assets and liabilities. Mark Glyptis, president of the ISU, said he saw a lot of positives in the purchase.

ISG would assume the company's $75 million debt, so in essence the entire mill would only cost $180 million. An announcement was made that ISG and the ISU were already working on a new contract. *Boy, wasn't that fast?*

So on February 26, papers were filed for the sale of Weirton Steel, called an Asset Purchase Agreement, for $158 million in assets and $97 million in liabilities. The proposed deadline for submitting bids was April 6. An auction was held on April 12 at 10:00 a.m., in Pittsburgh, Pennsylvania. *My father, rest in peace, would never have believed this even if he had lived to see it.* On the positive side, ISG reported a $24.9 million profit for the fourth quarter of 2003.

With the union now in the command seat, March began with the clock ticking with getting an agreement between the union and ISG. The outcome from this point forward, good or bad clearly rested on the shoulders of the union. Weirton management was essentially out of the picture until the actual documents were signed to let ISG take over control. Mark Glyptis said they were working night and day to get this done. I'm not so sure he needed to dramatize the situation. Remember Mark had the documents that the Weirton management team presented to the entire union executive committee several months earlier.

On March 3 (surprise) the ISU and ISG rendered a tentative deal. ISG would cut union job categories from 32 to five, thus allowing for more flexibility within the workforce. How creative, but this sounded remarkably similar to a deal that Weirton management presented to the union. Maybe our proposal lacked the same content, but it was definitely a proposal with the same structure and personnel changes.

ISG was now being challenged in court by a group of creditors. The sale was being labeled a "fire sale." Essentially it was. A new effort was started to try to bring Weirton out of bankruptcy, not by the company or the union, but by a group known as the Informal Committee of Senior Secured Noteholders of Weirton Steel headed by Mr. John Correnti. John D. Correnti had been the former CEO of Nucor Steel.

On March 16, a new labor contract was announced. It would be for five years and would reduce labor grades from 32 to five for production and maintenance workers and three labor grades for office, clerical, technical and professional workers. Hourly rates would be from $14 to $19.50 with raises at 12, 30, and 46 months into the contract. The contract would expire March 1, 2009. [3]

By the end of March, Weirton filed for another bankruptcy extension until June 30. The ISU ratified a new contract with ISG while Mark Glyptis claimed that he saw a different future with ISG. It meant major changes in the way the firm was operated. He said, "This ISG deal is a good deal and I think it's going to enable us to keep steel in the Ohio Valley for many decades to come." He stated, "I like the team-oriented philosophy and the idea that workers would be compensated according to performance, which typically is evaluated on a 24-hour basis. It's a very exciting concept for us and one I support totally." I wonder why he didn't embrace that philosophy when it was offered to him when Weirton's management team presented it for consideration. *Funny, how the grass seems greener depending on which side of the fence you're on.* [3]

Since ISG already had a senior IT executive on staff, and was not interested in me, I was left to decide my own fate. Without a lot of options, I decided to retire. So, on March 31, 2004, I cleaned out my desk and unhooked my computer. At a little before 5:00 p.m. I walked out of the General Office building for the last time. I retired after serving the company for 33 ½ years of dedicated and proud service. The following additional information is recapped from various outside data sources.

In early April, the groups trying to delay the sale of Weirton were all rebuffed by the bankruptcy court. There was talk of collusion, alleged in the ISG offer. Attorney's contended that ISG "front loaded the deal" as was reported by intercepted emails between certain company executives. But this was totally unfounded, without merit, and never proven.

On April 13, the auction was over. Weirton's Board of Directors studied the bids to make a recommendation to the bankruptcy court. On April 15, ISG cleared all antitrust issues. The next day, on April 16, the Board of Directors of Weirton Steel chose ISG.

On April 20, the bankruptcy court ruled that ISG won the assets of Weirton Steel with a bid of $237.5 million with a competing bid by the bondholders of $364 million being rejected by the court. After the bondholders filed an appeal, on April 30, the court came back quickly and gave the order to ISG.

On May 7, the Judges approved the Weirton settlement, and by May 20 the Weirton Steel Corporation, that was once home to thousands of men and women, ceased to exist. International Steel Group, Weirton Division, took over formal operation and named Manager Bill McKenzie to spearhead the leadership.

The chart shows the progression of 45 steel companies that went into Chapter-11 bankruptcy between 1999 and 2003.

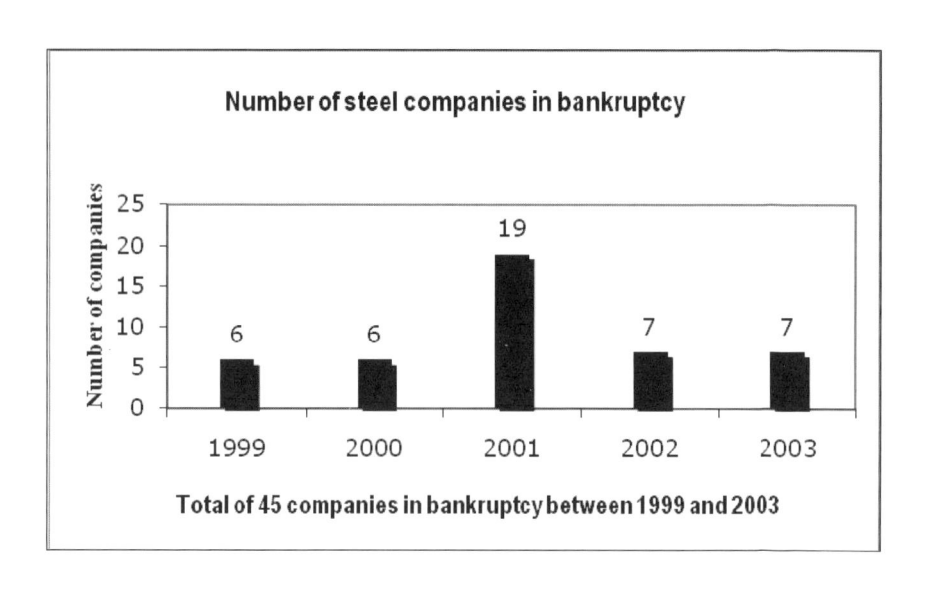

Number of steel companies in bankruptcy

Year	Number of companies
1999	6
2000	6
2001	19
2002	7
2003	7

Total of 45 companies in bankruptcy between 1999 and 2003

Chapter Eight - Epilogue

Fast forward to July 9, 2004, ISG announced that it would restart a second blast furnace. In a news release, Mr. Rodney Mott, CEO of ISG, painted a rosy picture of the mill's future, saying, "The integration of Weirton Steel into the ISG family of businesses had occurred seamlessly and more rapidly than we had expected." *Looks like a nice marriage has finally taken place.* Mott attributed the seamless transition of Weirton into the ISG group to the "enthusiasm and hard work of our employees and the cooperation of the Independent Steelworkers Union (ISU)," which agreed to a new contract that reduced jobs from 3,000 to 2,100. [1]

In that same article, Mark Glyptis again praised ISG's commitment to Weirton. "The brighter future I've often spoke of is within our grasp," Glyptis said. "We must keep an integrated steel mill in Weirton. It means so much to so many people, and this valley." I took away from his comments that it was like rubbing management's nose in the fact that "he" negotiated the deal: it was "he" that would now become the hero. In the end "he" would have the last laugh. [1]

Now fast forward again to April 12, 2005, nearly one year later. Mittal Steel from Calcutta, India with operations out of London, England, announced it was buying ISG for some $4.5 billion. *Boy, short marriage, I guess the honeymoon is over. Remember it's all about the money.*

Then June, 10, 2005. Eight weeks after Weirton had been absorbed by the Mittal Steel Group, the following statement was released to the media:

> Mittal Steel has announced a lengthier outage with accompanying layoffs, for its plant in Weirton, West Virginia.

The blast furnace had been idled for about 10 days and was to be reactivated this week. "However, the market conditions that led to the earlier decision haven't improved," said Bill Brake, Executive Vice President, United States Operations East.

"We've decided that it's better long-term for the business and for the Weirton plant and its employees to use the next few days to prepare the equipment for a longer outage. We'll bring it back up when the market tells me that the time is right." [2]

The shutdown of No. 1 Blast Furnace (No. 4 had already been idled earlier) had a nasty ripple effect. It forced the closure of the basic oxygen plant (BOP), which converts blast-furnace iron to steel, and the continuous caster, which makes molten steel into slabs. The number of employees on layoff grew from 370 to 700. [3]

Weirton's finishing mills continued to fulfill customer orders by using slabs shipped by rail from Mittal's Cleveland and Sparrows Point plants. Brake estimated that the outage would last between six and eight weeks. A return to full operations was expected between August 1 and 15.

But on August 19, 150 more steelworkers were furloughed, and rumors spread that Bill McKenzie had resigned. That evening WTRF-TV in Wheeling, informed its viewers:

"We have learned that the plant manager of Mittal Steel is stepping down. Bill McKenzie began overseeing the plant shortly after ISG bought the plant.... It is not clear why McKenzie is resigning. Union stewards were told late this afternoon about the resignation. McKenzie, unlike company heads before him, was well known for working inside the mill along with union workers, although he was management."

Stunned by these developments, the ISU came up with a plan for $93 million in cost cuts in order to reopen the hot end. The plan was submitted to Mr. Brian M. James, the new General Manager whom Brake had promoted from the finishing and shipping department at the Mittal Cleveland facility and who took over the job vacated by Bill McKenzie. Eventually, the information was relayed up the chain of command, from Brake to Mr. Lou Schorsch, CEO of Mittal USA, and, according to Schorsch, to Mr. Lakshmi Mittal, who was the founder, Chairman and CEO of Mittal Steel, and the corporate board, which included former ISG Chairman Mr. Wilbur L. Ross. [5]

It appeared the handwriting was on the wall. Demand for steel had fallen off, and there was a buildup of inventory at steel service centers. Mittal Steel was determined to work off the inventory by cutting production and stabilizing prices. This is where Weirton came in.

Unknown to Weirton workers, as well as to many ISU officials, Mittal Steel kept obsessive track of all financial aspects of its five integrated mills (Burns Harbor and Indiana Harbor in addition to Cleveland, Sparrows Point, and Weirton). The mills were compared and ranked according to their raw material inputs, manufacturing costs, and product profit margins. At the bottom of the list lay the "swing" plant – the facility that, in times of low demand, didn't generate enough money to please the steel-masters in London, England. That "swing" plant was Weirton.

Weirton was plagued by higher raw material costs, especially coke, than the other mills. The funny part was that no one from the union truly understood the overwhelming high costs of raw material, or how they impacted the hot end of the mill. The ore-pellet contract Mr. Mott negotiated with Cleveland-Cliffs under ISG, had committed Mittal to 14 more years of steelmaking at Weirton. This did not sit well with Mittal's management at all. [6]

Union politics also came into play. Weirton was the only plant that was not represented by the United Steelworkers of America (USWA). Before taking over ISG, Mittal Steel had entered into a "memorandum of understanding" with the USWA in which "the USWA agreed to support the merger and to waive its right of first refusal to acquire ISG under the ISG collective bargaining agreement." [7]

According to two sources, Mr. Lakshmi Mittal gave his word to USWA President Leo Gerard that the United Steelworkers would not be laid off unless and until non-USWA workers were dismissed. Mark Glyptis didn't have that kind of clout. His Independent Steelworkers Union didn't carry much, if any, weight at all. The ISU carried weight when Weirton was Weirton, but had nothing to bring to the plate to compete with the "big boys." Again, you have to remember Weirton was the swing plant.

So it was left to Brian James to break the news that Weirton Steel would no longer be making steel, as it had been doing since 1909. The November 29, 2005, announcement said that 800 union positions would be terminated as part of the shutdown of the hot end.

The announcement caused enough of a stir in West Virginia, where the mill was still the state's largest industrial employer, to force Mr. Schorsch to come to Weirton and address ISU members at the Serbian-American Cultural Center. Mr. Adam Townsend of the *Wheeling (W.Va.) Intelligencer* provided this account:

> Mr. Schorsch told about 1,400 ISU members that Mittal reviewed the $93 million cost-cutting package the union put together and found that it would not reduce costs enough to keep Mittal Weirton's hot-end operations open.
>
> "We reviewed it [the plan] in Chicago and, frankly, it wasn't enough," Schorsch said at the union meeting. "It didn't come out with enough improvements to make this a viable hot end.... [The plan] was looking at best-case scenarios versus what we see in the market and what we see in the marketplace and what we see other facilities can do."
>
> "We feel like we're heading into a very difficult market situation. I understand it's a very good mill. There's a lot of money that we've put into it. As a company, we've got seven hot mills. We don't have the demand to fill seven hot mills."
>
> The crowd was spilling out of the banquet-hall and the rank-and-file greeted many of Mr. Schorsch's responses to questions with "boos" and "catcalls."
>
> There was talk among union members at the meeting that because the ISU was unaffiliated, it was taking the brunt of Mittal's cost cutting, while the United Steelworkers members at other Mittal acquisitions would not loose their jobs.
>
> "If we were in the USWA, would we be in this position?" asked one ISU member.

Schorsch, however, answered these criticisms by saying the decision to shut down the blast furnace at Mittal Weirton was purely based on numbers – that is, economic viability. [8]

Schorsch outlined the future of Weirton as a tinplate finishing operation and said that the company was exploring the possibility of adding new equipment to the facilities. But he cautioned: these capital improvements are "not a slam dunk." He said he would promote at least the edge cutters and tension-leveling improvements to the tin mill to Mittal's board, the body that has the final say over capital expenditures. [9]

  The ISU met with West Virginia Governor Joe Manchin and U.S. Senators Robert C. Byrd and Jay Rockefeller. On December 15, Rockefeller issued a press release from his Washington office pledging to "hound" Schorsch "every day" until "we get a firm commitment about the future" of the tin mill. Boy, this was really something. If Senator Rockefeller felt that strongly where was he when Weirton was trying to merge with Wheeling-Pittsburgh Steel? *Politics at their finest!*

  Rockefeller was quoted as saying, "I'm extremely frustrated by Mittal Steel's decision to close the hot-end plant, and I made absolutely sure that Mittal's United States CEO, Mr. Schorsch, knew exactly how I felt." His webpage release concluded, "I will not stand by while Mittal plays with the lives of the finest steelworkers in the world. Weirton deserves better." [10] And again I ask Senator Rockefeller, where was he when the merger was trying to take place and why didn't he influence the outcome? *We'll see if the Senator's words impress Mittal Steel.*

  To appease Senator Rockefeller, Mr. Schorsch promised to assign General Manager Brian James to "reconfigure" the mill to make its operations both optimal and world class. In fact, by shutting down the hot end, Weirton would now become "more competitive in tin mill operations," an unidentified company spokesman explained. [11]

  On January 11, 2006, General Manager Brian James acknowledged that the number of laid off steelworkers had reached 950, but said that the additional cuts came from white-collar and support staff.

The 950 figure became the official number that Mittal disclosed under the Worker Adjustment and Retraining Notification (WARN) Act. [12)]

In February, Mittal USA offered ISU workers a "voluntary termination" buyout plan. They were given a choice of lump-sum payouts and a bonus, or extended health care and jobless benefits. Those with 20 or more years of service could take a $60,000 payment plus a $13,500 bonus, or supplemental jobless benefits and 30 months of healthcare coverage. Workers with between 10 and 20 years of service could opt for a $47,000 payment and the bonus.

Those who did not take a buyout and lost their job would be placed on a preferred hiring list. Depending on future production demands, the mill would have between 1,100 and 1,200 jobs available, according to the company.

Maybe in Mark Glyptis' mind he might have felt he joined forces with the wrong company. Maybe it wouldn't have been so bad to try and work with Weirton and Wheeling-Pitt's management to try and work a deal of our own, or forge a new company of our own.

To add insult to injury, Mittal shut down Weirton's Hot Strip Mill, rolling the last coil off the mill on December 27, 2007. A mill that cost the company over $500 million to renovate had come to a halt. Weirton Steel executives spent more money on this single facility than what ISG purchased the entire plant for, ($255 million).

As of May 2010, Mittal had not authorized any major capital investments into the tin mill as promised. I haven't heard any rhetoric from Mark Glyptis as was his custom when we were just Weirton Steel and he would "bash" Weirton management at the drop of a hat. I've heard no stumping or vocalizing to the news about the inter-workings of the mill, or how Mittal has essentially screwed Weirton.

It is this writer's opinion that it is just a matter of time before Mittal exhausts all of the resources in the tin mill and then closes the plant for good. Despite all the dedicated work and quality of product, sooner or later a large infusion of cash is going to be needed, and Mittal will just close the doors for good and steelmaking, the dream of so many for over a hundred years at Weirton Steel, will finally come to an absolute end.

Chapter Nine – Could the collapse have been prevented?

Weirton Steel started out as a company with a mission led by men and women that carried a vision of how not only to become successful, but to stay successful and grow. That concept was fully realized, time and time again, throughout nearly eighty years of steelmaking, until finally the boys at the top decided not to invest any additional capital into Weirton Steel, the flagship of the corporation. The division of National that made National Steel successful decided it didn't need Weirton anymore.

The politics were in the works for several years before this announcement, which shocked the valley, as men at the top became a little too greedy for their own good. Somewhere along the way, the concept of making high quality steel for a decent price, reinvesting in the people and equipment that produced the steel, while paying a fair wage to the workers, got lost in the shuffle. I believe once executives found ways to reward themselves, they caused an infection that spread through their cozy little world, and the people in the middle and at the bottom suffered and lost as a consequence. Once this so called "pocket stuffing" began, executives took their eye off running the company, events unfolded that caused problems to occur, and they started blaming others. Their focus was on self-reward and nothing more. Look at what has happened to nearly all of American businesses, especially the financial markets. Executives gave themselves huge bankrolls and bonuses and then they had the arrogance to ask the public and the government to bail them out. All the while, their boards fully supported their actions. *So what does that tell you of who's running America?* Their responsibility was to themselves while forgetting about everyone and everything else. The executives in the steel industry failed to realize their so called "glory" was founded on the men and women that turned the material into product and the product into profit.

When employees work their way through the ranks, learning, as they gain experience by solving problems, they become educated to the ways of a manufacturing facility. Learning from the so-called school of "hard knocks" is worth more than a formal education can provide, especially when dealing with manufacturing or steel- related jobs. Not that a formal education isn't helpful or important, but learning from real life experience in a working environment is unsurpassed.

Weirton Steel was founded on many great principles. One important principle in particular was integrity. Weirton Steel stood for integrity, not only to the community, suppliers, and customers but especially to the employees. Weirton Steel's reputation in the world market of manufactured steel was one of outstanding integrity and moral conviction. From men like E. T. Weir who started it all, to Jack Redline and his front line managers, they were all men of integrity. These men knew all the aspects of the steel industry and how to combat issues to keep it productive. That one element of being able to "walk your talk" was missing after the ousting of Bob Loughhead. Those who had the opportunity to work with Jack Redline and his front line managers know exactly what I'm talking about.
     In every company that is represented by a union there will always be issues of contention. Whether the issues stem from work rules, compensation, pensions or healthcare, common ground must be reached to keep the company stable and profitable. Management and union officials have an obligation as professionals to always keep the best interest of the company and the employees at the forefront of all their decisions.
     But, when this concept gets flawed, especially when management and union start drawing lines in the sand, when issues and problems go unresolved, the stage is set for impending failure. When the board of directors and executive management fail to plan for the future, and when obstacles that could impede the success of the company aren't addressed, a road of self-destruction begins. It always starts slowly and goes nearly undetected until some outside or inside event occurs. Then the company becomes totally unprepared to deal with the situation and everything becomes reactive.
     When Weirton first started, E. T. Weir hired the men and women with the skills needed to make the best product in the industry. By Weir's hand alone did men and women come from all parts of the globe to be made part of the Weirton Steel family. He took the time to surround the company with top quality employees, from the bottom to the top. He worked with executive management to create a business plan that kept the company afloat, even during perilous times. I believe the process needed to go beyond normal bounds, and with the board develop a business plan that included the anticipation of "what if" scenarios along

with corrective solutions so as to weather the worst of storms. Our corporate leaders at the top must realize they cannot do it alone, nor should they. They have to realize the heart and soul of any company are the men and women who produce and deliver the product.

However, during those times of exceptional need they must work together to build a business plan with realistic achievable goals. Weirton management and union were too often at odds with one another. So a workable business plan was almost impossible to develop. The board of directors had only minimal steel experience to foster a true business plan, and throughout my years I really didn't see a plan that was exercised to any degree of success. Seldom did the company hold anyone accountable or responsible for not achieving their goals. Look how many times between 1999 and 2003 that plans and goals were developed. Only a few of the goals were actually achieved because there wasn't follow-up or accountability.

It was obvious, to me at least, that a change in leadership needed to happen at some key positions within the executive and senior management levels, but that didn't happen. It was just status quo. People needed to be replaced when it was obvious that their performance was lacking, but everything was glossed over. I believe that even if the board did know, they probably wouldn't have done anything to correct the situation. In my opinion, a constant fight over "control" and "power" happened ever since the beginning of the ESOP and escalated after Herb Elish took the lead. So could the collapse and demise have been prevented?

What role did the Board of Directors play in the collapse?

Weirton Steel journeyed down the road of self-destruction with the overthrow of Bob Loughhead and the board appointment of Herb Elish to replace him. This started a long journey with inexperienced men with limited knowledge of how a steel mill was supposed to operate let alone how to make it profitable. These men, despite limited steel mill experience, had one main focus: they knew how to foster deals, not only for themselves but for their family as well, and they did it legally. I once heard Herb state something similar to: even a person who was commissioner of sanitation for New York City could run a steel mill. *Well, think again Mr. Elish.*

The main reason Weirton was profitable in the early years of the ESOP was totally due to the steel knowledge of the employees making the steel. This occurred under the leadership of Jack Redline, and was carried forward by Bob Loughhead. Despite the claims that Elish made regarding his contribution to Weirton Steel, he, in my opinion, was irresponsible in his duties by backing and approving spending hundreds of millions of dollars that produced no positive results and especially with no accountability. Programs that could have produced something positive where never followed through. Millions of dollars were spent anyway. Countless trips by executive management to the far corners of the globe were all paid for by the company. These trips returned little dividend to the company. Excellent insight into the "behind the scenes" working of the board can be found by reading Phillip H. Smith's book, *"Board Betrayal."*

Executive and some senior management individuals received extraordinary salaries. They took full advantage of everything and anything including bonus upon bonus for "performance" that was never truly realized. And so it went. The board of directors had a responsibility to oversee how the company was run and oversee those who ran the company. That never really happened with any degree of success. Maybe in a small sense it occurred because there were some board members that did have a genuine concern for the success of Weirton, but not as a collective board.

As mentioned earlier, the successful years at Weirton, when profit-sharing was common, were largely through the efforts of Bob Loughhead and other key individuals in mid-level management positions who allowed that to happen. When Herb Elish took over, it was still the momentum of Bob Loughhead and his team for which Herb took credit.

Too many key people either left the mill on their own will, or were forced to leave, and thus began a slow process that started to unravel the core essence of the mill. The new people never came close to filling the shoes of those who left. When the core elements were no longer there to provide direction and make key decisions regarding quality or production, or what to sell, the company started to come apart internally. As each thread started to pull apart, events started happening, business goals were missed, quality went down, defects went up and then someone started the "blame" game. This put everyone on the defensive and they begin to take their eye off the ball and started missing key indicators. The strategy of the company got twisted and everyone began grasping at straws, corporate direction changed in hope of improving the situation but nothing worked. Sometimes it becomes a slow process, like at Weirton, and the only thing left are to blame outside factors, like the economy or imports, anything to divert the attention away from the board and executive management.

That's where the board of directors needed to step in. The board needed to keep their eye looking at least two years into the future with business plans that should have produced results. If they were true experts as they claimed, then they should have been able to head off or avert steel's cyclical problems, maybe not entirely but at least enough to buffer the blow. But that was not the case at Weirton. We had people looking into the future but little action was taken by the board to avert those issues. So what did the board do to hold executive management accountable? Nothing.

One classic example that started it all was the IMIS (Integrated Manufacturing Information System) project. Phil Smith touched on this in his book but had a few of the specifics and details out of place. I can relate to this project because I was the project manager.

About a year after Bob Loughhead took the reign I submitted a letter explaining the concept that several of us had envisioned for Weirton Steel. This was a program that would eliminate the need to handwrite any production information ever again, allowing computers and barcode readers to manage the information on the plant floor. It would require a significant investment of capital because at that point in time there were no computers or network connections on any of the plant operating units. The exceptions were units that came with computers as part of the original equipment when the unit was purchased and installed

Our concept was simple. The large mainframe computer at the General Office had all the order information. Planners would look at those orders and decide how they should be run and in what order they should be processed. We would simply send this planned information to the computers on the plant floor operating units. Barcode scanners, similar to those in supermarkets, would scan a pre-existing barcode from each coil. A simple scan would verify to the entry-end operator that the coil was in fact the correct coil to process. That coil information would transfer to the delivery end of the line and, after processing the coil to customer specifications, a new barcode number would be assigned to the coil by the computer and the entire process would be loaded back to the mainframe computer. The coil would then head to the next operation. Since the mainframe computer kept track of all the numbers and customers, it knew exactly where in the plant the material was located. This process continued until the coil was ready to ship to the customer.

At any given time in the processing of the coils, a customer could see electronically where in the process cycle their coils were located. Knowing the location of the coil would determine the approximate time the coil could be delivered. This entire process would put Weirton in the forefront of the competition because no one else had the ability to do what was being suggested.

Unfortunately for me, this idea received much attention, including several calls from Bob Loughhead himself, but didn't have senior management's support. Only when Herb Elish came to the helm, after taking a blood bath in California at the Canners Convention, where customers beat him silly about on-time delivery, did he finally get the message.

The Canners Convention was a sounding board for companies that sold and purchased tin plate for commercial use. This very extravagant and pricey event was a place to socialize and do business at the same time. If there was dirty laundry to be aired, this was the place. This gave the companies and their senior officials an insight into how their company fared with their competition. This convention was important to companies like Weirton because it demonstrated what had to be done to improve their position in the market.

On his way back from the trip, Herb had befriended several individuals who represented a company call the Index Group. They explained to Herb that they had a new process called "reiterative engineering." They could develop software and the mechanics to complete a project in less time than had ever been done before. They could automate Weirton so that any customer would know where their coil was located within our plant and know exactly when it would ship. The concept, using a four-step process could cut development time dramatically. So the IT Director, two managers and myself went to Boston for two days to learn more about this process. Now the IT Department was in a full court press to try to get something moving.

In early December, we arrived in Boston, and after spending several hours with this group, I realized that this concept was not going to work in a steel environment. Maybe it would work in a less complicated environment but by no means a steel mill. I expressed my concern very vocally and adamantly and was asked to refrain from any more comments. The inference of the Index Group stating it could, under their direction, have the project up and running by September 4 was astounding. This was just nine short months away. It was ridiculous! This meant that the project needed to be scoped, priced, board-approved, equipment ordered, installed, software written and checked out and operational, by persons who knew little or nothing about our industry. *The only Person that could have pulled that off built the universe in six days and then rested on the seventh. I didn't see anyone with halos.*

However, not only did the Index Group get the lead role, but they also convinced executive management that Weirton IT employees could never pull off something that large in the timeframe suggested. We needed super powers, and people that could accomplish this feat only come from the outside. The Index Group got approval to sub-contract CSC or (Computer Science Corporation) from Falls Church, Virginia. As the weeks turned to months, we finally received board approval in February for a price of $5 million. But, just several weeks into the planning process, it was determined that the equipment was inadequate, the computers were not sized properly, etc., etc., and the price went to $6.8 million within a month. Now you have to understand that despite all the problems, nearly four months had passed, and the original project completion date of September 4 didn't move. So they were going to operationally install a system, on which no work had started, in a manner of five months.

Unfortunately nothing went as planned and nine months turned to a year, then two years. CSC was asked to change project managers, the scope of the project grew almost exponentially. Why? Because Elishs' outside experts didn't have a clue how complicated a steel mill was and so the true representation of what was needed was done later instead of sooner as it should have been in the first place.

The project came to a final blow when I caught the second project manager from CSC changing the project time lines early one morning in my office. I finally convinced my direct report, at that time Tom Evans, what was going on. I had a plan to take over the project and within six months we would have it operational, and by year-end fully implemented. I had several meetings with our legal counsel and several board members to lay out the plan and was given the go-ahead.

True to our word and the magnificent job of the Weirton IT employees, we showed everyone what we were made of. We didn't need the Index Group or CSC, we just needed someone who knew steel and how our processes worked. We rallied around our concept and believed we could be successful, and in the end, we were. The project came in slightly under $15 million, but took three years to complete, so it only put Weirton slightly in the forefront of the competition because by now everyone was following the concept we started. Yes, this was a lot of money, but I believe it could have been worst if I didn't step in when I did. I believe that if Bob Loughhead had remained at the helm of Weirton Steel we would have succeeded and beat the three-year window by less than half that time. [1]

The point here is that neither the board nor the outside experts knew how complicated a steel mill was. With a limited background in steel it was an up hill battle every time they approached a new idea especially one like IMIS. IMIS was an exceptional idea that was acted upon and placed in service by the people who supposedly didn't have the knowledge, and still continues to provide excellent information about our product to our customers.

When the board was approached with making a decision on the renovation of the Hot Strip Mill for some $500 million, I believe they approved it without proper due diligence. Why didn't they foresee the problems that a project of that magnitude might cause? The reason was they relied on their "so called" experts and went ahead and approved the enormous spending anyway. The Hot Mill project was 100 time's worse than the IMIS project. It was mismanaged, had cost over runs, and several law suits were filed. I'm sure a few questions were probably asked by the board, but the project manager was such a "spin" artist, it really didn't matter; they gave him free reign to do as he pleased.

Weirton Steel's motto seemed to be that if any outside company charged an exorbitant outrageous rate, they had to be good, so hire them. Weirton repeated that concept time after time and always received the same result; we paid them handsomely and received little in return.

The board owed a responsibility to the company and the employees to make the best decisions possible when it came to projects with a $500 million plus price tag. What due diligence was performed by the board to make such a decision? They failed miserably in their duties as board members. One of the reasons Bob Loughhead got ousted was he wanted a systematic approach to spending. He wanted a rational approach to modernizing. He wanted accountability on how money was appropriated. Herb Elish convinced the board to modernize aggressively, and Elish was the man for the job. Well, I guess hindsight wins. *I would have picked Bob.*

And once Herb Elish got his way, he put the wheels into motion. Some people today do not realize that as chairman, Mr. Elish had given his wife a title and position at Weirton. Although, she never served in that position, she was taken care of extremely well. In August 1992, Herb negotiated an employment agreement where he would receive payment of $7,500 per month for life while his wife received $3,750 per month for life. Also included was a provision that when Herb turned 62, he would receive $10,417 per month for life while his wife would receive $5,209 for life. All of this setup through annuities. The employment agreement was all done legally, with board approval. But, how many other annuities plans have been established and never disclosed? This all happened as part of doing business at Weirton Steel. This is a far cry from the principle of integrity and moral conviction that Weirton was founded on. So what did the Board of Directors really do for Weirton Steel? [1]

The most powerful position at the board level is the chairman. This position has to be one of utmost integrity and ultimately where the buck stops. The chairman has control over all aspects of the company but that surely wasn't the case with Weirton's board of directors. When Elish was at the helm he carved out a sweet deal for himself and his wife, while instituting special retirement accounts for the executives. All the while he sidestepped the part of holding executives accountable.

When Richard Burt took over, he was purely a passive non-aggressive chairman whose interest was not Weirton Steel. His presence at the board meetings, the ones I attended, clearly displayed a disinterest in the subject matter. There was no way he was going to get involved in the day-to-day operational issues of the company. So the board created an environment of dysfunction that eventually filtered into the executive and senior management ranks.

Let's look at the amount of revenue generated by this board and how that revenue impacted the bottom line since the ESOP was formed. It was under the leadership of board members, the chairman and executive management that an overwhelming number of losses occurred year after year beginning in 1990. The only exception to these losses were in years 1994 and 1995.

Let the reader decide if this "so-called" performance merited the tens of thousands of dollars paid to board members for their command decisions, or the millions of dollars that was paid to executive management, not including exceptional bonuses. The following graphs show net incomes since 1984.

Net Income Data 1984 - 1990
First 7 years Weirton made $26.3 million dollars
Average net sales of $1.2 billion dollars

Year	Net Income (Millions of dollars)
1984	2
1985	0
1986	-2
1987	12
1988	-2
1989	16
1990	0.3

Source - Weirton Steel Annual Reports

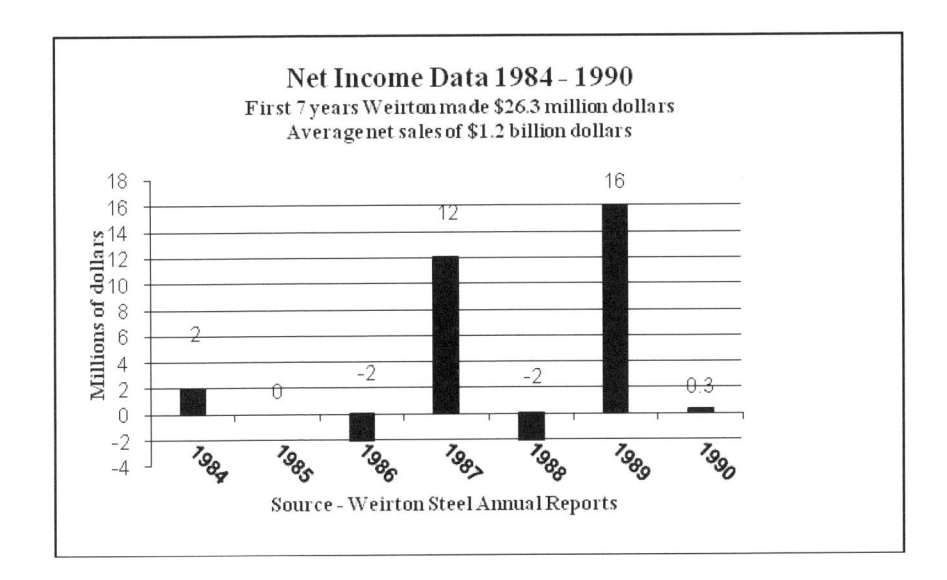

Despite the appearance of the small dollar amounts, these net amounts were after $314 million was contributed to the Employee Stock Ownership Trust and nearly $190 million paid out in profit sharing. The company made significant progress during the leadership years of Bob Loughhead between 1984 and 1987.

However, under the leadership of Herb Elish, something was seriously missing: revenue! Elish came on board as Chairman in 1987, and despite the upswing in revenue, I believe the momentum created by Bob Loughhead significantly impacted those revenue numbers, Elishs' claim to fame came after 1988. Having posted a $16 million profit in 1989, the company lost nearly $16 million in 1990, netting only $314,000 in profit. Revenue continued to decline until 1994 and 1995, and then the bottom fell away. Part of the profit in 1994 and 1995 resulted in money received from insurance from the 1994 fire at No. 9 Tandem Mill. It's all in the way you portray the numbers that makes it sound less problematic.

It had gotten so bad between 1991 and 1994 that a lawsuit filed in a West Virginia circuit court prompted the board and executives to spend nearly $7 million of the company's funds to purchase insurance that would protect them from the consequences of acts of gross negligence they committed.

Net Income Data 1991 – 1997
Second 7 years Weirton lost $320 million dollars
Average net sales of $1.2 billion dollars

Year	Net Income (Millions)
1991	-75
1992	-32
1993	-229
1994	35
1995	48
1996	-50
1997	-17

Source - Weirton Steel Annual Reports

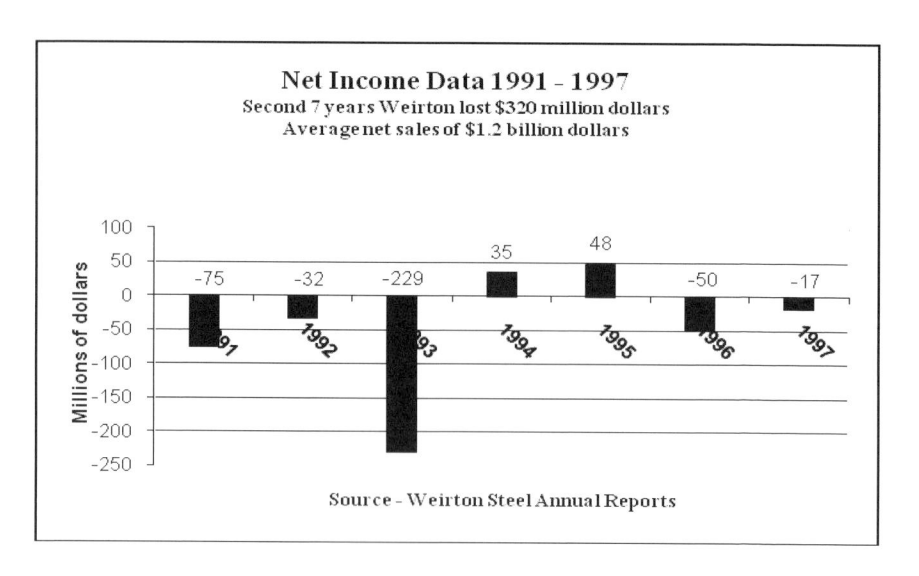

In early 1996, Richard R. Burt was elected Chairman of the Board of Directors. During the next eight years under his leadership Weirton Steel managed to lose an incredible $1.480 billion. *Fantastic job, Mr. Burt!!*

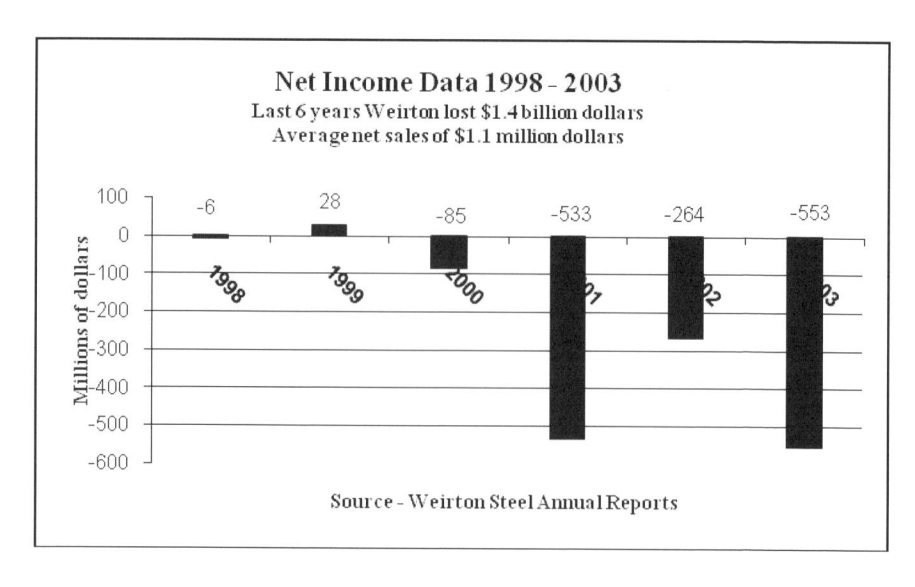

Net Income Data 1998 – 2003
Last 6 years Weirton lost $1.4 billion dollars
Average net sales of $1.1 million dollars

Year	Net Income (Millions)
1998	-6
1999	28
2000	-85
2001	-533
2002	-264
2003	-553

Source - Weirton Steel Annual Reports

When one looks at the background of the board it was clearly apparent that the only board member that had an actual background in steel manufacturing was Len Wise. The other members came from investment institutions, legal institutions, private enterprise or consulting firms. Without that steel manufacturing background, one limits the ability to understand the elements that can affect decisions. It is sad that Wise didn't come on the board earlier; things just might have been different.

Board members who were not officers or employees were paid an annual retainer of $15,000 per year; $800 for each regular board meeting attended; and $700 for each meeting of a represented committee. In 1999 annual retainers were increased to $25,000 per year with $10,000 coming in the way of common stock. [2] Mr. Burt received an annual retainer of $120,000 per year. [3] $10,000 per month for attending one four hour meeting once a month. *Oh, where did I gone wrong?*

What role did Weirton Steel Executive Management play in the collapse?

Weirton Steel's executive management group comprised those individuals that sported titles of vice president, senior vice president, or executive vice president, and represented the heads of the major departments within the corporation. These ranged from plant operations, engineering, human resources, legal, logistics, finance, purchasing, etc., to name but a few.

In some organizations the role and responsibility of Chairman, President, and Chief Executive Officer (CEO) is typically given to one individual, while other organizations split these responsibilities by having a Chairman oversee a President and CEO. This provides a more uniform reporting structure and represents a more even distribution of responsibility and power.

The executive vice presidents usually report directly to the President and CEO, and the CEO would in turn report to the Chairman of the board. However, in Weirton's case the President, CEO and Chairman was the same person,--initially Mr. Bob Loughhead and then Mr. Herb Elish. By the time Mr. Richard Burt took the position, it had already been split, and he held the title and position of Chairman alone.

Under the executive vice presidents were the senior managers and directors and managers of the various departments. These senior managers and directors were the "overseers" of the management team and the managers, mostly mid-managers. These managers supervised the employees that performed the various functions, the actual "workhorses" of each department.

Several departments played key roles when considering the performance at Weirton Steel. The first was the sales department because they represented the ability to secure orders from customers and set pricing to generate revenue. The second was plant operations because they represented the ability to produce these orders, to the highest quality possible, to satisfy the demands of the customer. These two departments needed to be in lockstep with one another. Any discord, on either side, interrupted the normal cycle of the company to perform and generate profit. Once a disruption occurred, the company could start losing orders, and the company would begin to decline.

Within Weirton there were generally two specific groups or categories: those in operations, and those in support and logistics. However, the largest department in Weirton Steel was plant operations. The vice president that controlled plant operations was truly the person in "charge." The Information Technology department that I was part of was a "support and logistics" group for Weirton Steel because it reached across all departments. These employees had a most difficult job trying to constantly balance or bridge the relationship with the plant operations management employees.

The plant operations management employees always felt the support and logistical group didn't understand the importance of their job. And, when it came to prioritization, the plant always took precedence. We never seemed to be able to find a middle-of-the-road way of working together. As a result, duplication of effort took place. This in turn wasted time and money because operations always convinced their executives that they had the solution, and the support areas didn't.

Not only was this concept untrue, it created a duplication of effort and cost the corporation millions of dollars. Considering the number of people, salaries, health insurance, and pensions, a large number of inefficiencies were created, all of which were approved by executive management. In addition to the people, an entire separate network of computers and servers was also approved for this group by executive management. *Not really a good way to run your ship.*

Prior to the ESOP, this contention between operations and Information Technology support was not an issue. IT support prior to the ESOP was provided by a division from National Steel. The National Steel employees were located in Weirton and developed some really dynamic and leading-edge technology projects in just about every department of Weirton Steel and never presented a problem. But after the ESOP, through a series of downsizings and layoffs, several internal groups approached operations and convinced them that they should be given the opportunity. It was at this point where the duplicity of effort started and was protected by the vice president of operations.

I started my career in the Tin Mill in 1970 but migrated to the Strip Steel area in 1974 as a systems engineer. I assisted in the start-up of the No. 5 Pickle Line. This is where I saw first hand the problem of having too many electrical devices that were incorrectly engineered into a production line. As engineers, we try to find ways to eliminate these devices because they provide little benefit and usually create constant maintenance nightmares. These electrical "gadgets" decrease productivity by causing delays, so we look for ways to eliminate them so productivity and performance can increase.

I was challenged with a similar situation on No. 9 Tandem Mill. Once the mill was officially signed over by National Steel to Weirton Steel, we could modify, change and eliminate whatever we wanted to increase productivity and enhance performance. I recall that before leaving the mill for another position, we removed nearly 100 electrical devices that were either under-engineered or installed because some engineer hadn't really thought about doing something a different way.

So, in 1988, when I was asked to be on a team with two other engineers to develop the specifications for the new hot mill renovations, I was extremely excited. I knew I would use the "lessons learned" confidence from the start up of No. 5 Pickle Line and No. 9 Tandem Mill to put together a specification that would minimize costly parts, equipment and technology that we didn't need. *Oh, the best laid plans of mice and men.*

However, changes began to occur shortly after the Hot Mill specification was written and negotiations began with the various contractors and vendors that were bidding on the project. I was very concerned that unnecessary items were going to be installed on the mill. I was fearful they would provide little or no benefit to the mill and result in maintenance nightmares.

I was also extremely concerned about how certain technologies were being selected. Although several concepts were reasonable, the technologies chosen were neither appropriate nor necessary to produce the quality of steel expected. It was the relationships that developed between the project manager and the vendors that I believe played a key role in selecting those technologies.

I was asked to sit through the negotiating process with the vendors, so as to limit their proposals to the specification guidelines. That's where I started to notice that the project manager began engaging in some sidebar negotiations after the formal meetings had taken place. After several weeks of this activity, I expressed concern that we were veering off course from our original mandate. We began adding additional equipment and technology that in my opinion was not needed. The cost was outrageous, so why put something in that wasn't needed? The project manager's reply was, "Don't worry about it."

After several more weeks passed, the project manager, Craig Costello, along with one of the engineers that helped develop the specification, seemed to be going down a path of no return. Technologies were being suggested that were never proven in an actual mill operating environment. Companies seemed to appear from nowhere with suggestions and proposals. Private meetings were beginning to take place after hours.

The concept of control had completely changed, and despite my complaining, I was overruled. I finally went to my IT director and asked to be removed from the project. I expressed my displeasure over how it was being run and stated that if left on its present course, it would end up costing millions upon millions of dollars needlessly. I stated that neither Craig nor the engineer were listening to any of my suggestions or realized the problem they would eventually create. I realized my presence in this case was futile. And so, the spending and buying continued. Over $500 million was spent needlessly and senselessly, and no one could stop them. The net result; Craig was eventually promoted to vice president of operations.

In the end, countless hours and manpower were utilized to refurbish the Hot Mill, and it did perform well, producing a high quality product, but not to the degree expected. Since certain technology and engineering models and equipment were never installed or implemented, hundreds of millions of dollars were wasted and the true potential of the mill was never realized.

The other engineer on the project eventually became the head engineer and went on to accomplish a great deal for the Hot Mill. As a computer and process engineer he was able to extract the most out of the technology that was purchased and installed. He was able to somehow make the critical pieces work together. He did a fantastic job right up to the very end. I consider him the best process automation engineer that came out of Weirton and I commend him for outstanding performance for all those years of unselfish dedication.

What Craig began to build within the operations areas was an empire. It had started to evolve several years after the ESOP, but really accelerated after Craig began calling the shots. He ruled by intimidation. During daily operational meetings, some of which I attended, when he walked in the room, one could hear a pin drop. There was never eye contact made with him, as you didn't want him to "unload" his temper. His verbalizing was limited to three or four letter words. His language was primitive. Even with women in attendance, it didn't matter; the dialogue and exchange was always the same: rude. And so a dynasty was slowly created and continued until he retired, and even continued to a lesser degree with his successor.

His actions did nothing for the plant operational groups other than placing fear in them. It was the worst, ineffective management style I had ever witnessed, but it impressed the executives and obviously the board.

As a result of Craig's actions, the plant floor and a number of support and logistic departments lost valuable employees that could never be replaced. That knowledge, once lost, could never be brought back. You could tell by the replacements that were hired that these new individuals really didn't understand steel. But, those who embraced his management style were in, and those who crossed him, were out. He had a number of followers within operations, all part of what I call the "good ol' boy" network. No one would challenge or argue with his tactics; those that did, only did it once.

An example of Craig's tactics was with the manager of the Total Quality Task Force. A total quality program is considered the most critical program in any manufacturing company. Without this program there are limited ways to control how the product is processed. Without control of the process there are limited ways to improve the product. One day the project manager was here, two hours later; he was gone. The program dissolved! *Oh, well, so much for quality!!*

Aside from the enormous expense at the hot mill, most employees or stockholders didn't realize Craig had requested permission to purchase a "sizing press" for the hot mill. He received approval by the board to move forward.

This sizing press was to have been installed at the front end of the Hot Mill after the reheating furnaces. Its primary purpose was to reduce the width of the slab to the proper customer order width size. The concept was to standardize width coming out of the continuous caster and use the sizing press to get the width to the final customer order size. The concept and benefit would have been great IF the sizing press was installed and IF the sizing off the continuous caster was fully developed. The problem was, before any of the logistics were completed to understand if the concept would work, the order was placed, and the money, over $25 million was spent. The sizing press is still exactly where it was unloaded, at the Weirton Steel Finished Product Warehouse. There it sits today, in a pile of rust, never installed. The work on the caster never materialized either.

Although the concept was fine in theory, the practical application was never developed. I helped to evaluate the cost of placing this piece of equipment into production. The cost was in excess of $40 million. Another classic case of the board and executive management not understanding what was truly involved. I believe as a result, Craig was promoted to Executive Vice President and Chief Operating Officer. Yet another example of a bad decision, no accountability, but rewards.

This "good ol'boy" network that was started at the board level was now being showcased within the plant operation areas and was thriving. So even with the best of business plans being prepared, if operations didn't like them, they would just ignore them. Instead of trying to build a working relationship with sales and operations, Craig built enormous walls that no one could get over, under or around. In the end, operations won.

Craig wasn't the only executive that walked away with millions of dollars, but he was the most visible and a hometown boy at that. More than a dozen other executives reaped similar rewards with varying degrees of magnitude. They kept mostly in the shadows.

As I sat, time after time, in long and drawn out meetings, with the same rhetoric over and over with the same result, I knew nothing was going to change. It was like the definition of insanity, doing the same thing over and over and expecting a different result.

The "good ol'boy" network continued on, and no one wanted to stop it. Executives just buried their heads in the sand so they didn't have to deal with it. I believe it was a primary reason we could never reach our goals. Nothing changed.

What role did the Independent Steelworkers Union play in the collapse?

The Independent Steelworkers Union (ISU), were the unionized workers, men and women, that performed the work of making and producing the highest quality of steel in the world. Organized in 1933, and formally recognized in 1951, this union at one point in time represented nearly 13,000 workers.

I started my career as a union laborer in the Tin Mill in 1970, so I could relate to both sides of the fence, union and management. I could appreciate what some employees had to deal with being in the union. For most, it was very rewarding. The work some chose was their specialty, and they preformed their work with great expertise. Some had a natural talent and could perform just about any job in the mill, while others, aspired to perform specialized work like being a roller on a mill. Most of these skills were acquired by learning from someone who did the job for years on end, and who in turn had learned "on the job." These skills could not be learned or taught in any school. Some refer to these skills as "skills of hard knocks" because that's how they were learned, and once learned they weren't easily forgotten.

Being in the Union had both positive and negative aspects. The positive was clearly "strength in numbers," and always having a sounding board on working conditions, pay raises, benefits, and the like. On the negative side, or positive side as some might see it, a union member was nearly impossible to fire or remove from the ranks. The union always protected their members, regardless of the issue. I believe a union member always had the upper hand. The sad part that I witnessed, time after time, was when an employee needed disciplined for not performing his/her job or came to work under the influence of some substance, the union always protected that individual no matter how serious the situation was, to the determent of the company as a whole.

When poor performance affects quality and several attempts to fix it don't work, the employee must be let go for the good of the company, not retained because of seniority. Protectionism can only support a person for so long, and at some point effective leadership must rule in favor of the company. That didn't happen.

I felt the union played a role in the demise of Weirton on several fronts. First, the union president Mark Glyptis had some type of resentment for management in general, regardless of what a person knew or what a person did for the good of the company. I'm able to make that statement after working with and being associated with other former union presidents. They always tried to meet somewhere in the middle of the road and work toward bridging differences, not towards alienating management.

After Mark was elected union president, I had the opportunity to meet him for the first time at one of the weekly IMIS review meetings. These meetings had been held for several months, as we worked through how the IMIS project was going to affect the number of jobs on the plant floor. We had been working with the former president, Virgil Thompson, and had made considerable progress; then the elections came, and Mark was elected. With any automation project, especially the size and complexity of IMIS, certain job consolidations or eliminations were needed. All the changes needed to be discussed and worked out with the Union.

Mark began that first meeting by introducing me to the new union executive committee, as the person that would bring Weirton to its knees. This, I believe, stemmed from the fact that he knew little to nothing about technology, and how it could play an important part in putting Weirton ahead of our competition. I had tried to extend to Mark a way for us to work together to get the best from both worlds, as this project was inevitably going forward. There was constant tension, and we never got to a point where I felt confident that we were accomplishing our goals.

On the flip side of that statement, I'm reminded of one exchange with a certain Vice Chairman of the Union Executive Committee, only several months previous to this meeting. We had just begun our layout of the IMIS project and were now ready to discuss the number of impacted union positions. As my plant floor technical manager and I were about to sit at the large table on the top floor of the union hall, and the vice chairman loudly stated that if we came to discuss union eliminations, he would throw us through the window. I immediately moved toward the window and raised the blind, suggesting that I didn't want to take this with me as I was being propelled through the window. At this point, he began ranting and cursing and told us to "get the f*^* out of the union hall, and don't come back!"

We went back to the General Office, and I called the union hall to talk to Virgil. I explained that as painful as this process was, we had to at least start a dialogue. He said he would talk to the vice chairman and call me back. Within the hour Virgil called and asked that I come to the union hall at 11:30 a.m. as the vice chairman wanted to sit and "break bread."

When I arrived I was pleasantly surprised that this gruff, hardcore, rough-talking steel worker, the one that could always be identified by a sock hat he wore, was standing next to a table with several loaves of fresh Italian bread and an assortment of salami and cheeses. This was his way of making peace, and we literally sat and broke bread. As lunch turned to late afternoon, we walked away with a sense of slight accomplishment as we started a long road of give and take. That was true negotiating. That was something that I never saw in Mark.

Mark seemed to have a real disdain for Herb Elish, Dick Riederer and especially John Walker. He seemed to resent something about them, maybe his own fear of their position or authority. There seemed to be an unwillingness to work with them, to find common ground solutions anywhere. Regardless of the situation or circumstance, Mark seemed to fight tooth and nail over even common sense items. When he didn't get his way, he would run to the press. It appeared Mark enjoyed his name in the spotlight, where he provided public bashings of management on a regular basis.

And so it was with Mark's lack of cooperation to help find ways to curb or cut costs to help the company when it was in total despair and trying to find ways to avoid bankruptcy. Mark knew how desperate the company was and how unstable its financial situation was. You would think that when management was ordered to give up both wage and health care cuts, a similar offering would be discussed from the union. But those talks never happened. I felt those health care cost concessions, from several thousand Union employees, would have provided enough cash to help the company stay liquid over that rough period when it needed all the cash it could get. Even though the union managed to find ways to help reduce certain costs, in a number of different areas, I felt the health care area would have provided the biggest help in achieving our revenue demands.

Secondly, I will never understand why Mark and the union executive committee didn't act responsibly after we presented an almost similar company restructuring plan to the ISG plan that the union eventually accepted. Repeated attempts to bring something to the table, or to at least break bread, never happened. This inaction on his part led me to believe that Mark somehow wanted to show his constituents and everyone else that he was an intelligent mastermind. That he and he alone was able to bring management skills and union savvy to the table and come up with a solution to raise Weirton out of the ashes. I believe his inability to discuss a new company, similar in design to what was happening at ISG, helped push Weirton down a slippery path that led to the collapse of the entire company.

When union and management are unable to at least discuss issues openly, and decide to resolve issues independently, the entire moral structure that the corporation was built on collapses. Regardless of the situation, professionals needed to work toward the common good of the company. It is a give and take process. Union and management need to realize they can't always win everything they want; there has to be compromise.

I recall how one great steel man did the job. His name was Jack Redline, twice President of Weirton Steel. When he was president, Jack and the union worked through their issues together. He would sit nearly every morning at the old downtown bus terminal on Main Street, over breakfast, and talk to the men about the issues, openly getting their feedback, their ideas, and feeling what was in their hearts. He took this information back and worked to bring resolution to the issues. Weirton continued to succeed. Union and management can solve their issues, but only if both sides are willing to put forth an honest effort: to sit down, trust one another and be able to "break bread."

I worked and had a personal relationship with other ISU Presidents. I believe that we worked toward meaningful and rewarding goals. However, that wasn't the case with Mark. It was as though he had a self-fulfilling prophecy to bring management to their knees, and at some point go it alone, so he could prove he could do it without management. I know by the union's actions and willingness to be acquired by ISG, he was leaving the control to someone else. I don't know the promises that

Mark negotiated with ISG, but I hope he is satisfied with the outcome and what is yet to come.

A union carries with it certain clout to help force issues out into the open, whether it is the operation of the board, or executive management, or the company not realizing its goals. A union can set and chart a course to hold these entities responsible, but that never happened. There were several lawsuits that would have certainly held board members and executives accountable for their actions, but the union backed away from those proceedings. This was especially true for the Hot Mill renovation project. I'm really not sure why they decided not to push the issue.

Finally, the union played a critical role as a member of the Finance and Strategic Planning Committee on the board of directors. What's amazing to me was how few times the committee actually met.

The strategic planning committee was to develop the plan the corporation would follow that includes:
a) projections of the market and competitive environment;
b) assessment of the Company's core strengths and weaknesses;
c) identification of key opportunities and threats; and
d) articulation of the Company's long-range direction, including action plans addressing both the core business and growth opportunities.

The committee in 1998 and 1999 met one time. How much could be accomplished in one meeting and during a critical period: the import crisis? [2)]

In 2000, three meetings were held, and in 2001, just two years prior to the bankruptcy, the committee again only met once. The Finance and Strategic Planning Committee consisted of Mark Glyptis, along with eight other board members. What truly was accomplished since it was apparent that none of the plans ever materialized? What goals did they set? Could anyone produce a plan or even an outline of a plan? I believe the answer is "no" to all the questions.

If this committee was truly on the ball, wouldn't it have known that since previous plans were never accomplished that maybe a change of tactics was in order? What follow up was ever done? What do you accomplish in one meeting? What this committee failed to produce is inexcusable. This was a $1.2 billion a year company with no set goals and no business plan to speak of, all of which was controlled by a key committee of the board of directors. The fact remains that nothing meaningful materialized from this critical committee!

What role did West Virginia's Congressional Officials play in the collapse?

West Virginia had three individuals that represent the interests for the Great State of West Virginia; U.S. Senators Robert C. Byrd and Jay Rockefeller and Congressman Alan Mollohan. These gentlemen were elected by the people and were supposedly dedicated to serve the people. They have been in office for a combined 104 years.

I fully appreciate all that these men have done for the state of West Virginia but I feel that here again when power and politics takes over, sometimes common sense vanishes and errors in judgment occur. Every politician makes fantastic promises at the onset of their campaign and, if elected, they almost never follow through with any. However, the most vocal side of a politician comes after an event that has already occurred that he couldn't influence. Historically politicians enter on the coattails of the situation, never at the beginning. In the case of steel imports, how much data was needed before action was taken? How long before you pick up a phone and ask for a meeting to discuss the issue? How long before a remedy is made and those at fault penalized? How long before action is taken to enforce laws that are already on the books? Why did it take so long to levy penalties on companies that were dumping steel into our markets?

When I mentioned that our representatives were always reacting instead of acting, I referred to the comments from Senator Rockefeller, who was "devastated" hearing that the hot end of Weirton would be shut down. He stated he sent some strong language in Mittal's direction. Are our congressional representatives that far out of touch with us that they couldn't see this coming? I doubt the Senator's words really had an impact on Mittal's executives …… they shut it down anyway. We need congressional leaders to work within the confines of the state of West Virginia and go to Washington when it's absolutely necessary, not the other way around. Just think of the millions we would save.

In the case of the merger between Weirton and Wheeling-Pittsburgh Steel, how many meetings did our legislative leaders hold with each company? ….. None that I'm aware of. How many meetings occurred with the Steel Board? I believe our political representatives' lack of timely questioning of the Steel Guarantee Loan Board caused them to issue their decision prematurely. Remember: the Steel Board denied the original loan application of Wheeling-Pittsburgh Steel just two months prior. Our leaders should have paved the way for that merger to take place, but that opportunity has been lost forever. The decision by the board was possibly made without having all the facts. Our leaders should have been on top of the situation every step of the way, but that wasn't the case.

In my opinion, our representatives needed to explain to the Steel Loan Board that legal and financial steps to join the companies together were nearly complete. If the committee had even the slightest doubt about awarding the loan, the board should have denied it and allowed the consolidation to move forward. As I indicated previously, I'm not advocating or suggesting that any illegal maneuvering should have taken place. However, a clear presentation of all the facts should have been presented to the board prior to its finalizing their decision.

Our representatives should have been on top of the entire situation on a daily basis. This was extremely important to thousands of employees. So, where were our representatives? My discussions of the situation with John Walker and Mark Kaplan indicated our elected representatives were on-board and highly informed as to the possible opportunities involved. I find that extremely difficult to believe in light of the outcome. The Steel Board ultimately voted in favor of granting a $250 million loan to Wheeling-Pitt. Since the Steel Board rejected a similar application, what changed their mind in just two months? With that single decision, the merger was off between Weirton and Wheeling-Pitt. Now no one will ever know what the two companies could have produced together.

I personally think that after an elected official serves more than two terms he/she begins to feel invincible and begins taking things and situations for granted. Even before two terms have expired, relationships, and contacts with special interests groups and lobbyists transpire. The concept of "by the people, for the people" somehow gets lost, and now it becomes "for me, and about me." As for this writer, I'm in favor of setting term limits on all our congressional leaders, not just in Washington, but the states as well. Sometimes changing the guard is beneficial. Replacing the old with the young fosters new ideas. How many new ideas have been realized from our congressional leaders? Answer that question before you cast your next vote!

      I cannot for the life of me understand why someone else from this state, with a population slightly under two million people, couldn't do their job and do it more responsibly? How do they represent our interests in Washington? Where do they place the needs of West Virginia businesses? How many new businesses have been brought to West Virginia since they took office? What part did our elected officials play in bringing Weirton Steel to its demise? So many people, spent countless hours, and effort to try and avoid a bankruptcy situation. Others spent countless hours creating a merger opportunity between two companies. There was limited support and effort from our congressional leaders to aid in these endeavors.

Chapter Ten – Lessons Learned

My good friend, mentor, and executive vice-president, Mr. Tom Evans was a person I tremendously admired. He provided me with a lot of valuable insight during my tenure with the Information Technology (IT) Department. The IT Department reported to him and he reported to the executive group. Tom's job was Vice President of Materials Management. He had responsibility for all material purchased throughout the corporation. He also had the added responsibility of the IT Department in the early years of the ESOP.

My relationship with him was upfront and personal especially when I assumed the role of IMIS project manager. As we started down this road his advice to me was quite simple; after each successful or unsuccessful project milestone was reached, perform a "lessons learned" exercise. You need to look at the things that went right and those things that didn't, and come up with lessons to help prevent repeating the same mistakes. These lessons learned outcomes became a very valuable and powerful tool for me. They helped me tremendously throughout my career.

The most important lessons learned were always "keep it simple." Similar to what our President John Walker once said, "If you're going to fail, fail fast, fix it, and then move on." I remembered doing similar exercises when I worked on the plant floor as an engineer but not in such an involved way. I always wanted to know just how successful or unsuccessful our efforts had been.

In the case of this book, I wanted to conclude with certain events that unfolded since the time of the ESOP and especially in the years leading up to the bankruptcy. Events, that if altered just a little, might have led to this book not being written in the first place. So here they are:

Lesson 1: Always place people around you that offer strengths to your weaknesses; that way everyone can become successful.

Lesson 2: If at all possible, split the office of the Chairman, President and Chief Executive Officer into individual positions. This will offer better balance and control, where power and responsibility can be equally shared, making sure they have industry-related experience.

Lesson 3: Hold the people on the board of directors, executive, and senior management accountable, and make sure they perform to the highest degree and with the highest integrity. If necessary, do it as a shareholder of the company. Leadership starts at the top, so make sure that what comes down from the top can be embraced by those who have to do the work at the bottom.

Lesson 4: First and foremost, bring integrity, moral conviction, trust and honesty to the position you have been given responsibility for and expect the same from those around you. Treat everyone with respect and assist wherever you can in helping others become successful.

Lesson 5: Encourage the building of a strategic business plan that drives and guides the business at all times. Identify those conditions or elements that can throw the business off track, and for every anticipated event have a corrective solution to at least minimize the circumstance. Develop an annual "lessons learned" from how the plan actually performed, and what was or wasn't accomplished.

Lesson 6: Lead by example. Learn from history and your past mistakes. Set a direction never to repeat past mistakes. Hire the best employees and re-invest not only in the company, but the employees.

Lesson 7: Hold all elected officials accountable for their decisions and actions. If they fail to uphold your expectations, vote them out. Encourage elected officials to meet a minimum of twice yearly with your company to understand your particular business and the problems it might be facing.

Lesson 8:   Strive to understand union official's points of view while holding them accountable for their decisions and actions as well. Union and management have to work together and agree what is best for the company and the employees. We all have to learn how to "break bread." No one can or needs to do it alone.

   We need to search our souls and try to hear the little voice inside to help guide us in our roles, actions and decisions.   We have to learn how to "walk our talk." We have to lead by our convictions and be humbled by our actions.   Trusting in yourself is one thing, but you also have to trust in the Lord to help guide your actions, and in the end those actions will be the correct ones, regardless of the outcome. Do what is right!

In Closing:

I saw the beginning of the collapse occur after the board of directors ousted Bob Loughhead and put Herb Elish into power. It continued a downward spiral with Richard Burt. I saw a board made up with members that possessed limited steel or manufacturing background try to run a steel company. I saw the board make one bad decision after another without much forethought or afterthought. I saw the board reward irresponsible behavior, bad decisions and incompetence. I saw executive management pay little attention to how the company was actually being run or how it should be run. I saw one arrogant executive force extremely knowledgeable people out of the company and rule with intimidation to satisfy an ego. I saw sales and operations develop an indifference that should have been stopped by either executive management or the board, but was ignored by both. I saw the operations department create their own support function causing duplicity of effort that cost the company millions of dollars, year after year. I saw the union develop resentment for management personnel in general, and an extreme unwillingness to work with executive management specifically. I saw the union so heavily burdened with their resentment they chartered a course to define their own future without consideration for the "cause and effect" it would have on the corporation as a whole and "all" its employees in particular. I saw a systematic process unfold that stripped away integrity and moral conviction. It was replaced by greed, power, and control that lined the pockets of the board and key executives. I saw our elected officials with their heads in the sand, nearly impervious to our plight, allowing our company leaders to practically go it alone, and then retaliate with disgust when our situation collapsed.

It was to a point of being almost criminal to see how these conditions unfolded and were carried through by those at the top. So many employees worked numerous hours to try and make the company a better place, trying to reach their goals, despite the fact that the cards were stacked against them. With no voice of recognition at the top, our efforts were doomed. It was a select few who had control and power over the rest. They strangled the life out of those who could have truly made a difference and possibly see Weirton succeed. For some, the handwriting was on the wall and they left for greener pastures and became highly successful as a result. For the rest, we tried with every ounce of strength we had, but we failed.

In the final days of Weirton Steel, a combination of internal events and circumstances prevented us from implementing anything significant from a so-called strategic plan or realizing any meaningful goals. A strategic plan developed in one sitting, once a year and then left to sit on a shelf to collect dust did us little good. Neither the board nor our key executives put forth any meaningful effort to find alternative solutions to help derive success from some of our most critical areas affecting the company. Little effort was put forth by the union to work with management to help realize and achieve success in areas that truly would have made a significant financial difference.

These events were paired with a series of sequential events involving our government and its inability to react quickly enough to steel imports. Taking four years to enforce our import laws in and of itself is criminal. Couple all of this with a genuine disinterest by our congressional leaders to understand what exactly Weirton needed to merge with Wheeling-Pitt, and it all led the way for Weirton Steel to end nearly 100 years of steelmaking.

When you look at all those so-called expert board members and executives that for years took millions of dollars out of our pockets to prosper their own wealth, it is obscene and should be punishable by law. Some of these people wouldn't understand the meaning of integrity. They came in, manipulated the rules so they could make extremely large sums of money, had so-so responsibilities, were never held accountable, and then they left, all because it was just business. But, when they say, "business is business" it is a term for them to rape and steal from the company while doing everything legally, and then they laugh all the way to the bank, set for life. For the rest of us, we now have to struggle for the rest of our days. Somehow, something went terribly wrong!

So, could the collapse have been prevented? You decide!

About the Author:

Thomas Walter Zielinsky was born in Steubenville, Ohio on December 28, 1946 and was raised in New Cumberland, West Virginia; the oldest of three sons born to Walda A. (Zumer) and Walter A. Zielinsky. Thomas graduated from Oak Glen High School in 1964 and attended West Virginia University for two years studying Electrical Engineering. He left school and enlisted in the United States Army in 1966 and was honorably discharged in 1969. Having served during the Vietnam War era, he was a member of the Air Defense Artillery Nike Hercules Missile unit, 100th Artillery Group, 5th Region Air Defense Command, where he achieved the rank of Specialist 5 – E5. After leaving the Army he worked as an electronic technician for General Dynamics Electronics Division in Rochester, New York on the F-111-F series fighter jet performing electrical testing, troubleshooting, and programming for the on-board computer systems.

Leaving New York, he was hired by Weirton Steel Corporation in 1970 as a general laborer and worked vacation turns in the Tin Mill electronic shops. He left the Tin Mill in 1974 and transferred to the Strip Steel Department as a salaried Electronic Systems Engineer on the No. 9 Tandem Mill. He worked a variety of salaried positions within the Strip Steel Department and eventually was promoted to Manager Process Control in 1983 just prior to the Weirton ESOP.

He held a number of different management positions, including Director of the Information Technology Department, where he ultimately became Senior Director in 1999 until his retirement at the end of March 2004.

He holds an Associate Degree in Electronic Engineering from the Capital Radio Engineering Institute, a Bachelors Degree from West Liberty State College and a Master of Business Administration Degree from the Franciscan University of Steubenville, Ohio.

A special thank you to all those individuals who assisted me with proofreading and making numerous suggestions; my deepest and most heartfelt gratitude to all of you. To Richard Pflug Jr. and Jane Melville of Tri-State Printing for all your assistance and guidance. Finally, a very special thank you to Mr. Rick Smith, historian, and video photographer for providing me with the "1952" photo for the cover and the key photo's to complete the center section of this book.

This is the author's first book.

References and Endnotes

General

Source for the majority of reference data, information, facts, statistics, employee numbers, reported profits and losses, and all other general information specifically have come from the website – AISTsteelnews.com/Weirton Steel News Achieves. My daily notes then supplemented the information from the above website for each year represented in this book.

Introduction

1) Stand Up For Steel, ISU Update, Quote – info@standupforsteel.com, WebWeaver Productions ohio@1st.net

Chapter One

1) History of Weirton Steel – www.weirtonmuseum.com - 100 years of Steelmaking
2) A Historical Timeline
   - In 1911, Mr. Weir acquired the 12-unit plant of the Pope Sheet and Tin Plant Company in Steubenville, Ohio. Annual output of tin plate surpassed that of all but one other company.
   - In 1913, a new cold rolled strip plant was being built and in 1915 – 1916 not one but two hot mills began construction.
   - On August 1, 1918, on Mr. Weir's 43rd birthday, the company was reorganized as the Weirton Steel Company.
   - In 1919, Weirton Steel was nearly complete in constructing the No. 1 Blast Furnace.
   - In 1920, seven Open-hearth furnaces, a 40-inch Blooming Mill, 18-inch and 21-inch Continuous Rolling Mills were commissioned into operation.
   - In 1923, Weirton built a Sinter plant and began building a Sheet mill plant and its first Coke plant.
   - In 1926, construction on the No. 2 Blast Furnace was started.
   - In 1927, Mr. Weir received financing for a new continuous 48-inch Hot Rolling mill in the Strip Steel Department to produce tin plate and hot and cold rolled sheets. This was the first mill of its kind in North America. Weirton Steel was always considered the pioneer of innovation and actually led the world-wide steel industry in technology and creative concepts. Also being installed, during this period, was the No. 11 Open hearth.

- In 1929, the depression year, Mr. Weir led a merger of Weirton Steel, Michigan Steel Company in Detroit, and the M.A. Hanna Company of Cleveland to form National Steel Corporation with Weirton as its key division. E. T. Weir became president of National Steel and John C. Williams became president of Weirton Steel.
- In 1930, the mainland Coke plant added 25 additional ovens and a new Structural mill was being installed.
- In 1933, the employees held a strike from September 26 to October 1, the only time in history that a strike actually occurred at Weirton. During this same time period the No. 4 Tandem mill had started construction.
- In 1936, the first Bessemer Converter was put into operation and the former Clarksburg plant was closed. (*A Bessemer converter was the first inexpensive process of mass production of steel and the prelude to the Basic Oxygen Furnace that came some 30 years later*). That same year Thomas E. Millsop became president of Weirton Steel.
- In 1938, the No. 5 Tandem mill was placed into operation.
- In 1940, the No. 4 Tandem mill became fully operational within the Strip Steel Department.
- In 1941, the No. 3 Blast Furnace was blown into service and the No. 2 Temper mill was added to the Tin Mill facility.
- In 1942, new tin lines were being constructed in the Tin Mill with No. 1 went into operation.
- In 1943, No. 2 went into operation. During this same period of time special equipment was installed at the Strip Steel department for rolling copper-clad steel for 30-caliber and 50-caliber shell casings for the war effort.
- In 1944, the No. 2 Continuous Pickle line was added.
- In 1946, the No. 3 Electrolytic Tin line was being installed.
- In 1947, No. 2 Blast Furnace was enlarged, and a total of 106 new Coke ovens became operational. The Strip Steel Department saw the No. 6 Tandem mill become operational along with renovations to the Hot Strip mill to increase its width from 48-inchs to 54-inches
- In 1949, four new Annealing furnaces began operation in the Tin Mill. The No. 1 Open Hearth ranked as the largest in the industry and began setting outstanding production records. The No. 1 Continuous Pickle line was placed in operation.
- In 1950, a new 61 oven Coke battery went into operation as well as the start up of the No. 4 Electrolytic Tin line, which, at that time, was the world's fastest tin plate facility.
- In 1952, the No. 4 Blast Furnace was placed into operation.
- In 1954, Thomas E. Millsop became president of National Steel and E. O. Burgham president of Weirton Steel.

- In 1955, the Hot Strip mill added a new 54-inch rougher, and the No. 1 Sinter plant was placed into operation.
- In 1956, the No. 7 Tandem mill was placed into operation in the Strip Steel department.
- In 1958, the No. 8 Tandem mill was placed into operations.
- In 1960, construction of the General Offices and National Steel Research and Development Center was started at the south end of Three Springs Drive.
- In 1962, the No. 2 Weirlite mill became operational in the Tin Mill.
- In 1965, construction work began on the Basic Oxygen Plant (BOP) and the No. 6 Electrolytic Tin line became operational along with the No. 5 Galvanizing line in the Sheet Mill. The Basic Oxygen Plant (BOP) became operational and was brought on-line with two of the largest steel making vessels in North America, representing 360 tons of steel making capability per vessel.
- In 1968, a Continuous Caster was placed into operation which put the company at the leading edge of steel manufacturing. The combined technology of the BOP and Caster set Weirton apart from the rest of the steel producers from around the world.
- Throughout the years, Weirton Steel installed state-of-the-art mills and facilities in just about every department. This single act of re-investing and re-modernizing the company kept Weirton as a true leader of steel manufacturing. Innovation in tin mill products was the corner stone of Weirton's success beginning in 1938 when the first 10-inch pilot Tin line was installed. In 1942, Weirton along with DuPont introduced the first halogen tin process and commissioned the ground breaking of No. 1, No. 2 and No. 3 Continuous Tin processing lines. In 1950, the No. 4 Tin line was commissioned and was, as stated earlier, the fastest and most consistent quality product tin line in the world. In 1955, the Hot Strip mill was modified, once again, to produce a more consistent 54-inch wide material.
- In 1971, Granite City Steel Company merged with National Steel. In 1973, the first continuous tension controlled pickling facility went into production in the Strip Steel department with the commission of No. 5 Pickle line.
- In 1975, the first continuous, fully hydraulic, computer controlled, 5-stand double high, No. 9 Tandem Cold mill was commissioned into service. This mill became a true leader, in its own right, incorporating technologies from Japan and Germany that combined to form a mill not equaled anywhere in the world.
- On March 2, 1982, a sad and shocking day developed for Weirton Steel and all of its employees. On that day, National Steel made a devastating announcement; it decided to limit future capital investment in the Weirton division.

- On September 23, 1983, Weirton employees approved three ballot items by a margin of nearly 7 to 1 to create the Weirton Steel ESOP with the employees giving up nearly 32 percent of their pay and benefits to forge Weirton ahead. Weirton Steel was now the largest ESOP in the United States.
- On January 11, 1984, documents were signed between Mr. Howard P. Love of National Steel and Mr. Robert L. Loughhead, former Copperweld Steel president and now Weirton's new Chief Executive, forming the nations largest ESOP. Weirton had a total workforce of 7,844 employees. [3]
- In 1986, the first profit sharing occurred on March 14 in which $20.3 million was distributed to the employees. In 1987, profit sharing at the 33 percent level saw $15 million distributed to 8,345 employees. In 1988, profit sharing was $40.2 million; in 1989, $75 million, and in 1990, $21.8 million was distributed to the employees. The employees shared over $172 million during this five (5) year period. [3]

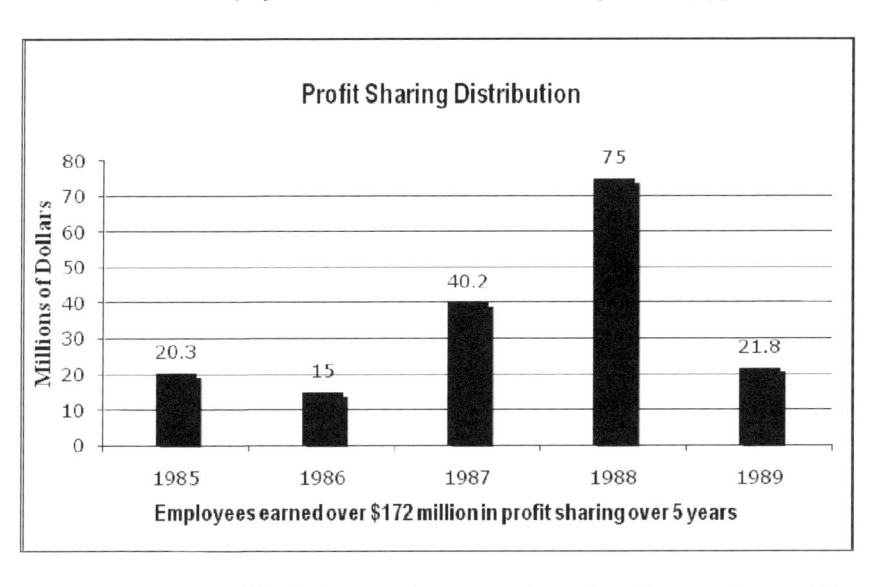

Profit Sharing Distribution

Year	Millions of Dollars
1985	20.3
1986	15
1987	40.2
1988	75
1989	21.8

Employees earned over $172 million in profit sharing over 5 years

- In 1989, Weirton employees voted to relinquish some shares of the company stock in an initial public offering (IPO) to finance a five-year $500 million capital improvement program.
- In 1989, the largest re-modernization was done to the Hot Strip mill in the Strip Steel department.
- In 1994, a second IPO was necessary to shored up debt incurred in modernizing the plant.

Profit Sharing Distribution

Year	Millions of Dollars
1994	17.6
1995	24.2
1996	0
1997	0
1998	0
1999	16

Employees earned $57.8 million over 6 years

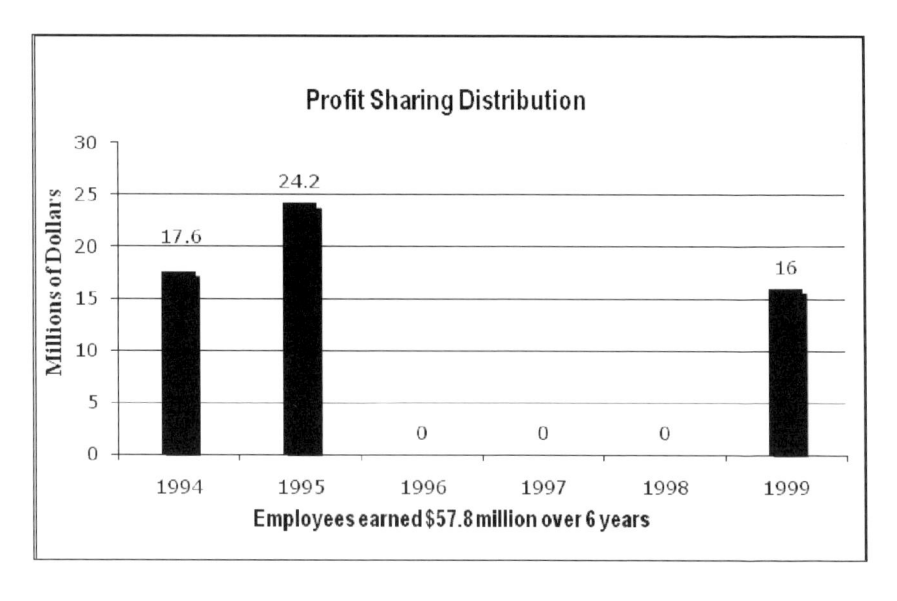

- April 6, 1994 another major event occurred when the No. 9 Tandem mill caught fire and was out of commission for over 6 months.

2) 1984 – Weirton Steel Annual Report
3) 1986, 1987, 1988, 1989, 1990 – Weirton Steel Annual Reports
4) 1994, 1995, 1996, 1997, 1998 – Weirton Steel Annual Reports
5) 1996, 1997, 1998, 1999 – Weirton Steel Annual Reports

Chapter Two

1) Data360.org, Iron and Steel Imports
2) Stand up for Steel, ISU Update – info@standupforsteel.com, WebWeaver Productions ohio@1st.net

Chapter Three

1) Data360.org, Iron and Steel Imports

Chapter Four
1) www.stewartlaw.com
   Section 201 of the Trade Act of 1974. Sometimes U.S. industries and their workers find themselves overwhelmed by rapidly increasing imports. This may flow from a number of factors having nothing to do with international price discrimination (dumping) or subsidization. Since 1930's, U.S. law has provided the possibility of seeking temporary relief so the companies and their workers can either regroup or execute an orderly retreat from the market. If a domestic industry is either seriously injured or threatened with increased imports a substantial cause of the injury, the law calls for the U.S. International Trade Commission to recommend to the President relief designed to prevent or remedy the injury and assist the industry in adjusting to import conditions. The President has discretion whether to follow the recommendations, provide alternative relief or deny relief. Relief granted is of limited duration and degressive (meaning it will decline over time, consistent with the concept of temporary relief to help an industry and its workers adjust to the new conditions of completion). [1]

2) Weirton Steel Business Plan 2002, dated November 2001

Chapter Five
1) Weirton Steel internal document Restructuring Update, January 14, 2002
2) Weirton Steel Proxy statement, November 6, 2002 – Proposed Charter
- The existing corporate charter contained highly restrictive supermajority and other voting provisions, unique to Weirton and, as originally intended, effectively prevent an outside investor from obtaining control. (This supermajority voting language was adopted into the original charter to prevent anyone from taking control of the company and would require 80% of stakeholders, which included union and management personnel and certain outside investors to provide approval to any offer. This language was referred to as a supermajority vote.) In addition, our authorized capital was limited and inadequate to fund any acquisition or investment strategy. It was extremely important to vote in favor of the necessary changes if Weirton had any intention of succeeding with its strategic restructuring plan. [2]
- The board of directors unanimously approved the contingent charter proposals. These proposals were designed to provide Weirton with an adequate capital structure and governance arrangements more typical of a well capitalized, publicly held corporation.

- The implementation and effectiveness of the new charter was contingent on and subject to future events and action by our board of directors. Approval of the contingent charter proposals would not take effect unless the board, by a vote of 90% of the directors, approved an acquisition or investment by Weirton, which constituted a "transformative event." Critical to our board approval were the terms of the acquisition, the new investment, and the collective bargaining agreements that affect the union employees. Such an acquisition by Weirton would ultimately have to be approved by the board. The existing provisions of our charter would remain in full force, including the supermajority voting and other protective provisions. 2)
- A "transformative event" does not mean a purchase or takeover of Weirton by a domestic or foreign steel producer. If the board were to approve such a proposal to acquire Weirton, the supermajority vote of at least 80% of the eligible voting power of holders of our common stock and Series A preferred stock would still be required, notwithstanding stockholder approval of the contingent charter proposals. 2)
- The Board of Directors had defined a "transformative event" to be one which meets **each** of the following tests described in paragraphs (a), (b) and (c) below:
    a) a person or group obtains a controlling interest in the company (defined to be beneficial ownership of at least 50% of the voting power or sufficient percentage ownership of our voting stock to elect or control the majority of our Board of Directors) through an equity or equity-linked investment, the proceeds of which are used directly or indirectly to finance an acquisition or investment, or a series of acquisitions or investments, described in (b) below; and
    b) the acquisition of or investment, or a series of acquisitions or investments, whether effected by merger, consolidation, purchase, lease or other transfer of assets, in (x) businesses or assets which are used in the business or making, processing or distributing steel products, including tin mill assets, or (y) related businesses where the acquisition or investment is consistent with the company's strategy to focus primarily on higher margin, value added products, or (z) in businesses or assets which would result in a reduction of the company's operating costs, or a combination of the above; and
    c) the transaction or transactions described in clauses (a) and (b), as presented to the Board of Directors for approval, include terms that require, as a condition to the completion of such transaction or transactions, the person or group acquiring a controlling interest in the company to enter into collective bargaining or similar labor agreements for a period of not less than three years from the date of the completion of the transaction or transactions, covering at least 80% of all represented employees of the company, on terms that are reasonably acceptable to such employees, or at the discretion of the

- collective bargaining agent to agree to be bound by existing labor agreements. 2)
- Advance stockholder approval of the new charter was necessary to allow the company to be recognized as a credible acquirer in the marketplace and, importantly, to act quickly to take advantage of a particular acquisition or investment opportunity that the board determined to be in the best interests of the company's stockholders, employees and other stakeholders. Decisive and rapid action was particularly required to take advantage of assets purchased from bankrupt steel producers.
- In addition to amending our charter, there was a proposal to reduce immediately the size of the board from 14 to 9 persons. The "new" board would consist of 5 independent directors, 2 management directors and 2 union directors.
- Finally, a change would occur to allow an increase in authorized capital, an increase in the authorized capitalization of the Company from 57,500,000 shares; consisting of 7,500,000 shares of Preferred Stock and 50,000,000 shares of Common Stock to 275,000,000 shares, consisting of 25,000,000 shares of Preferred Stock and 250,000,000 shares of Common Stock.

3) Weirton Steel internal document Strategy Presentation, December 16, 2002
4) Weirton Steel Stockholders Notice of Annual Meeting, dated November 6, 2002
5) Weirton Steel internal document 2003 Business Plan, December 11, 2002
6) Weirton Steel internal Revised Business Plan December 14, 2002

Chapter Six
None

Chapter Seven
1) Steel analyst Chuck Bradford, from the Bradford Research/Soleil Securities in New York, January 16, 2004
2) *Weirton Daily Times*, February, 5, 2004
3) Courier-journal.com/business/news, Vicki Smith, Associated Press, March 30, 2004, "Weirton Steel Workers OK Pact With ISG"

Chapter Eight
1. ISG Press Release, July 9, 2004
2. ISG Press Release, June 10, 2005

3. "Mittal Steel Extends Weirton Blast Furnace Outage, *Steel News*, June 10, 2005
4. Shauna Parson, "Mittal Latest," posted on WTRF website, August 19, 2005
5. Strange Case of Weirton Steel by Mark Reutter April 25, 2006
6. Strange Case of Weirton Steel by Mark Reutter April 25, 2006
7. *Form 20-F, 2005 Mittal Steel Co. NV*, submitted to U.S. Securities and Exchange Commission, pg. 105
8. "Mittal Chief: No Hope for Plan, " *The Intelligencer*, December 14, 2005
9. Ibid.
10. "Rockefeller Meets with Mittal steel USA CEO," Senator Rockefeller's webpage, December 15, 2005.
11. Scott Robertson, "Mittal Tells Weirton Plant: Tin Is In, But Furnace Out," *American Metal Market*, December 15, 2005
12. WARN requires companies with 100 or more employees to provide 60-days advance notice of plant closings and/or mass layoffs.
13. "Union Details Buyouts at Mittal," *Pittsburgh Tribune-Review*, February 23, 2006
14. Steel analyst Chuck Bradford, from the Bradford Research/Soleil Securities in New York, January 16, 2004
15. Weirton Daily Times, February, 5, 2004
16. Courier-journal.com/business/news, Vicki Smith, Associated Press, March 30, 2004
17. Strange Case of Weirton Steel by Mark Reutter April 25, 2006

Chapter Nine

1) Weirton Steel Corporation, Proxy Statement May 11, 1992, page 10 & 11
2) Weirton Steel Corporation, Proxy Statement April 23, 1999, page 12
3) Weirton Steel Corporation, Proxy Statement November 6, 2002, page 9

Key Officers, Executives and Managers

Board of Directors 1984 ESOP

Robert L. Loughhead – Chairman, President & CEO – Former President of Copperweld Steel Corp
Harvey L. Sperry – Partner, Willkie Farr & Gallagher
Phillip H. Smith – Chairman – Smith, Yuill & Co. Inc.
Richard F. Schubert – President, American Red Cross
David L. Robertson – Partner, Volk, Robertson, Frankovitch & Anetakis
F. James Rechin – Vice President & General Manager, TRW Aircraft Components Group
Eugene J. Keilin – Partner, Lazard Freres & Co.
Lawrence M. Isaacs – Visiting Professor of Business Practices & Vice Chairman Susquehanna University
Gordon C. Hurlbert – President & CEO GCH Management Services, Inc.
Herbert Elish – No listing
Irving Bluestone – University Professor of Labor Studies, Wayne State University, Retired Vice President International Law, UAW
Walter F. Bish – President Independent Steelworkers Union

Board of Directors prior to 2002 reorganization

Richard R. Burt – Chairman – DILEGENCE LLC – Washington, DC
Michael Bozic – Private Investor – Pittsburgh, PA
Robert J. D'Anniballe, Jr – Managing Attorney – ISU
George E. Doty, Jr. – Private Investor – New York, NY
Mark G. Glyptis – President – Independent Steelworkers Union
Ralph E. Reins – Chairman & CEO – Qualitor, Inc. – Southfield, MI
Robert S. Reitman – Principal – Riverbend Advisors – Gates Mills, OH
Richard E. Schubert – SVP – EXCN Inc. – LaJolla CA
Thomas R. Sturges – Private Investor – New York, NY
John H. Walker – President & CEO – Weirton Steel
Ronald C. Whitaker – President & CEO – Strategic Distributions – Bensalem, PA
D. Leonard Wise – Former President & CEO – Carolina Steel – Greensboro, NC

Board of Directors after the 2002 reorganization

Richard R. Burt – Chairman – DILEGENCE LLC – Washington, DC
Michael Bozic – Private Investor – Pittsburgh, PA
Robert J. D'Anniballe, Jr – Managing Attorney – Union – *(Ted Arneault, President & CEO of Mountaineer Race Track and Gaming Resort replaced Mr. D'Anniballe in August 2003)*
Mark G. Glyptis – President – Independent Steelworkers Union
Mark E. Kaplan – Senior Vice President Finance and Administration & Chief Finance Officer
Thomas R. Sturges – Private Investor – New York, NY

John H. Walker – President & CEO – Weirton Steel
Ronald C. Whitaker – President & CEO – Strategic Distributions – Bensalem, PA
Wendell Wood – President and Chairman, United Land Corporation

Key Executive and Senior Management

Richard K. Riederer – Chief Executive Officer CEO
John H. Walker – President and Chief Operating Officer (Effective 3/21/00)
Craig T. Costello – Executive Vice President (Retied 4/1/00)
Earl E. Davis, Jr. – Executive Vice President - Commercial
David L. Robertson – Executive Vice President – Human Resources & Corporate Law
Narendra M. Pathipati – Senior Vice President – Corporate Development & Strategy
Thomas W. Evans – Vice President – Materials Management
Michael J. Scott – Vice President – Sales and Marketing
Edward L. Scram – Vice President – Operations
William R. Kiefer – Vice President – Law & Secretary
Frank G. Tluchowski – Vice President – Engineering & Technology & Restructuring Officer
Mark E. Kaplan – Senior Vice President Finance and Administration and Chief Financial Officer (CFO)
Richard W. Garan – Assistant Treasurer
Robert Fletcher – Controller
Patrick B. Stewart – Chief Information Officer (CIO) and Vice President

Key Corporate Senior and Mid-Management Individuals

Gregg Warren – Public & Governmental Relations & Corporate Spokes Person
Jim Gibbons – Director of Corporate Strategy
Thomas W. Zielinsky – Senior Director IT Strategy
Michael Biela – Director Software Development IT
David Lammers – Director Operations and Network Services IT
Howard Snyder – Director Plant Operations
James Ritz – Internal Audit and Year 2000 Project Manager
Harry DeVilling – Human Resource Manager for Information Technology Department
Jane Neal – WEIRTEC Project Manager – Polymer Coating
Donald W. Simmons – Manager Total Quality Task Force
Ken James – Hot Mill Design Team member, Project Engineer & Senior Automation Engineer Hot Mill
Robert Vidas – IMIS Plant Floor Technical Manager
Brian Wilson – Hot Mill Design Team member and Project Engineer

Other Key Individuals

Virgil Thompson – Former ISU President and Corporate Law and Economic Development
Walter Bish – Former ISU President and Labor Relations

Dominic Tonacchio – Former Vice Chairman of the ISU Executive Committee – (sock hat)
Kathleen Gennuso – Senior Account Executive Technical Solutions Hudson Global Resources
Jack Redline – Twice former President – Weirton Steel Corporation
Paul Mooney – Executive Vice President and Chief Financial Officer – Wheeling Pittsburgh Steel Corporation
Ted Arneault – President & CEO of Mountaineer Race Track and Gaming Resort – Chester, WV (Appointed to Board of Directors August 2003)
Len Anthony – Chief Financial Officer International Steel Group
U.S. Senator Robert C. Byrd
U.S. Senator Jay Rockefeller
First District Congressman Alan B. Mollohan
Brian James – General Manager Mittal Weirton
Bill McKenzie – Former General Manager Mittal Weirton
Rodney Mott – CEO International Steel Group
Wilbur L. Ross – Chairman International Steel Group
Bill Brake – Executive Vice President, Mittal Operations East, USA
Lou Schorsch – CEO Mittal USA
Lakshmi Mittal – Chairman Arcelor-Mittal International

List of Bankrupt Steel Companies

2003	2002
Bayou Steel (1/23/03) Kentucky Electric Steel (2/6/03) **Weirton Steel Corporation (5/19/03)** Slater Steel (6/2/03) WCI Steel (9/17/03) Republic Engineered Products (10/6/03) Rouge Steel (10/24/03)	Geneva Steel (1/25/02) Huntco Steel (2/4/02) National Steel (3/6/02) Calument Steel (3/19/02) Birmingham Steel (6/4/02) Cold Metal Products (8/16/02) Geneva Steel Holdings (9/13/02) Geneva Steel's parent
2000	**2001**
J&L Structural Steel (6/30/00) Vision Metals, Inc. (11/13/00) Wheeling-Pittsburgh Steel (11/16/00) Northwestern Steel and Wire (12/20/00) Erie Forge and Steel (12/22/00) LTV Corp. (12/29/00)	CSC Ltd. (1/12/01) Heartland Steel (1/24/01) GS Industries (2/7/01) American Iron Reduction (3/23/01) Trico Steel (3/23/01) Republic Technologies (4/2/01) Great Lakes Metals (4/11/01) Algoma Steel Inc. (4/23/01) Freedom Forge/Standard Steel (7/12/01) Precision Specialty Metals (7/16/01) Excaliber Holdings Corp (7/18/01) Laclede Steel (7/30/01) Edgewater Steel (8/6/01) Riverview Steel (8/7/01) GalvPro (8/10/01) Bethlehem Steel (10/15/01) Metals USA (11/15/01) Sheffield Steel (12/7/01) Action Steel (12/28/01)
1999	**1998**
Geneva Steel (2/1/99) Qualitech Steel SBQ (3/24/99) Worldclass Processing (3/24/99) Gulf States Steel (7/1/99)	Acme Metals (9/29/98) Laclede Steel (11/30/98)